MW01630269

TWA

KANSAS CITY'S HOMETOWN AIRLINE

TWA
London
MAP
TWA
THE LINDBERGH LINE
Fly the Finest...
FLY TWA
TRANS WORLD AIRLINES
COAST-TO-COAST IN THE U.S.A.
AND IN EUROPE · AFRICA · ASIA
ADMINISTRATION BUILDING, FAIRFAX AIRPORT, KANSAS CITY, KANSAS
TWA
DOUGLAS Luxury AIRLINERS
powered by
WRIGHT CYCLONE ENGINES
TWA
"The Lindbergh Line"
SHORTEST ROUTE
COAST TO COAST
109—Municipal Airport, Kansas City, Mo.
TWA
TWA Airline Hostess
TWA Color-foto

TWA
The
TRANSCONTINENTAL
Airline
ROUTE OF THE STRATOLINERS

TRANSCONTINENTAL & WESTERN AIR, INC.
SHORTEST FASTEST COAST-TO-COAST
TWA
The TRANSCONTINENTAL Airline

TWA
TWA
13
73699

THE LADY THAT NEVER GROWS OLD

TRANSCONTINENTAL
& WESTERN AIR, INC.
TWA
FASTEST COAST TO COAST

In Flight with TWA
JETSTREAM*
Newest . . . Finest
in the skies!
The luxurious
long-range Jetstream
can take advantage
of the smooth winds
of the upper-air,
the jet stream, flying
quietly with exclusive
synchrophased
(anti-vibration)
propellers, surely with
electronic-eye radar.
*Jetstream is a service mark
owned by TWA exclusively
TWA
TRANS WORLD AIRLINES
U.S.A. · EUROPE
AFRICA · ASIA
—remember your trip with pictures.

TWA
TWA
TWA
TRANS WORLD AIRLINE
PRINTED IN U.S.A.

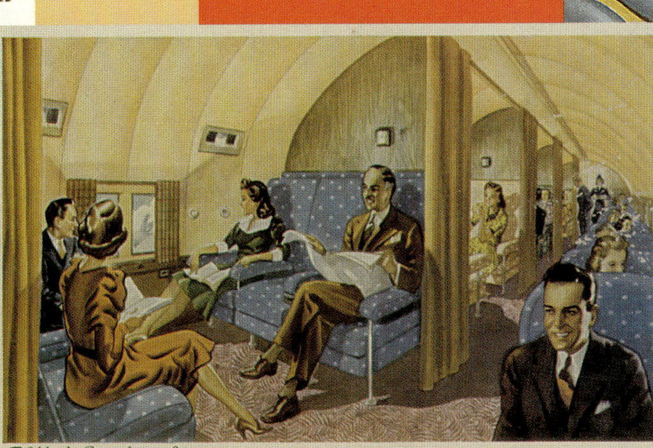
TWA Stratoliner Luxury

TWA
HE · LINDBERGH · LINE

**TWA: Kansas City's
Hometown Airline**

Authors: Julius A. Karash and
Rick Montgomery
Editor: Doug Weaver
Design: Barbara Hill-Meyer
Graphics: John Sopinski

Published by KANSAS CITY
STAR BOOKS
1729 Grand Blvd.
Kansas City, Missouri, USA 64108

All rights reserved
Copyright © 2001 The Kansas City
Star Co.

No part of this book may be
reproduced, stored in a retrieval
system or transmitted in any
form or by any means electronic,
mechanical, photocopying,
recording or otherwise, without
the prior consent of the publisher.

First edition
Library of Congress Card Number:
2001088602
ISBN: 0-9679519-9-2

Printed in the United States of
America by Walsworth Publishing
Co., Marceline, Missouri

Requests for permission to make
copies of any part of the work should
be mailed to StarInfo, c/o The Kansas
City Star, 1729 Grand Blvd., Kansas
City, MO 64108. To order additional
copies, call StarInfo (816) 234-4636
and say "Operator." Or visit our Web
site at www.kcstar.com

ACKNOWLEDGMENTS

The Kansas City Star set out to explore TWA's history and its local impact in early 1994, when many analysts wondered if the airline could survive the year. The newspaper's efforts culminated in a four-part series published in July 1995, the text of which is reprinted and expanded upon in this book.

Ever-tenacious TWA rebounded for a time. However, news of American Airlines' proposed buyout in early 2001 spurred Kansas City Star Books to produce this updated salute to the hometown airline. Many TWA loyalists, such as Marie Trainer, Tom Perry and Tom Dunn — son of the late TWA executive Ray Dunn — moved quickly to provide memorabilia, snapshots and artifacts, which were photographed by *The Star's* Johnna Flahive for these pages.

In addition to records drawn from *The Star* library, excellent advice and archival material were provided by the local Airline History Museum, the Special Collections Department of the Kansas City Public Library, the Truman Presidential Museum & Library, the Kansas City Museum and the Western Historical Manuscript Collection, University of Missouri-Kansas City.

The writers are indebted to scores of TWA retirees, one-time executives and airline experts who kindly submitted to interviews, often in their homes. Kathy Woodward, manager of the Final Approach Pub near the TWA overhaul base, introduced us to a lively group of TWAers who shared their thoughts one Friday afternoon.

These books were enormously helpful:

Air Line Pilots Association, *The Making of an Airline.* New York: TWA Pilots Master Executive Council, 1981.

Donald L. Barlett and James B. Steele, *Empire: The Life, Legend and Madness of Howard Hughes.* New York: W.W. Norton & Company, 1979.

George R. Bauer, *A Century of Kansas City Aviation History.* Historic Preservation Press, 1999.

A. Scott Berg, *Lindbergh.* New York, G.P. Putnam's, 1998.

Robert W. Rummel, *Howard Hughes and TWA.* Washington: Smithsonian Institution Press, 1991.

Dan Reed, *The American Eagle: The Ascent of Bob Crandall and American Airlines.* New York: St. Martin's Press, 1993.

Robert J. Serling, *Howard Hughes' Airline: An Informal History of TWA.* New York: St. Martin's Press, 1983.

Trans World Airlines Flight Operations Department. *Legacy of Leadership.* Marceline, Mo.: Walsworth Publishing Co., 1971.

TWA Clipped Wings International, *Wings of Pride: A Pictorial History,* compiled and edited by Gwen Nebelsick Mahler, Mary Lou Axcell Finch and Marie B. O'Connor Trainer; written by Donna Steele. Marceline: Walsworth Publishing Co., 1985.

Finally, the writers owe much to their brethren at *The Star* - including the current aviation writer, Randolph Heaster - whose coverage of TWA over the years kept the city informed and made this book possible.

— *Julius A. Karash and Rick Montgomery*

TABLE OF CONTENTS

DEDICATION

Kansas City Star Books dedicates this commemorative work to the thousands of TWA employees in Kansas City, past and present, who devoted their hearts and lives to shaping the face of commercial aviation. Because of their earnest work, TWA will forever, rightfully be known as Kansas City's Hometown Airline.

 # 'IT WAS A TIME'

Across the young face of Charles A. Lindbergh spread his patented hero's grin - sly and certain, but so slight as to reveal just a wisp of pearly white. Lindbergh wore the grin as he pressed a button on the California governor's desk. ✳ *A continent away, one bell dinged and a lightbulb flashed in New York's Pennsylvania Station. A band struck up "California Here I Come." A trainload of passengers began to roll west to Columbus, Ohio, where two Ford Tri-Motor airplanes awaited them in a field.*

By 1929 standards the event was dazzling. The beloved Lindbergh, only 27, had signaled the world that all systems were go: Transcontinental Air Transport was in business and its clunky contraptions could take off. New Yorkers for the first time could reach the West Coast in 48 hours by riding trains or buses at night and planes in daylight.

It meant landing nine times, including a 2:47 p.m. stop in Kansas City, Missouri.

It meant sweating through your best dress. And packing cotton in your ears. And praying that the winds stayed calm. And bouncing in a way that prompted wisecracking workers to tag the airplanes "vomit comets."

So began an adventure that assumed

many names, but in time everyone would know it by three red letters.

TWA.

As technical advisor to Transcontinental Air Transport, Lindbergh mapped that first cross-country route himself. The trip cost $352, roughly the price of a Model A coupe.

Aviatrix Amelia Earhart was among 10 passengers on the maiden flight of *City of Columbus*, one of the westbound planes christened that day. A car company executive named Edgar Gorrell sat nearby, awestruck. Nine thousand feet above the continental divide he wrote:

"I have just looked down upon lava beds and into extinct volcano craters and observed scenery as mankind never before has seen it."

Those passengers also witnessed the birth of what generations of Kansas Citians would call their "hometown airline."

PIONEERING AVIATORS LENT THEIR NAMES AND ADVICE TO TRANSCONTINENTAL AIR TRANSPORT, FORERUNNER TO TRANS WORLD AIRLINES. CHARLES LINDBERGH (RIGHT) HELPED MAP ROUTES AND VOTED TO PUT TWA'S HEADQUARTERS IN KANSAS CITY. ATCHISON, KAN., NATIVE AMELIA EARHART (BELOW) RODE THE INAUGURAL CROSS-COUNTRY TRIP AND PENNED A COLUMN FOR WOMEN PASSENGERS.

DIGNITARIES CHRISTENED "THE KANSAS CITY" IN 1929 BEFORE IT TOOK OFF FROM THE LOCAL AIRFIELD JUST NORTH OF THE MISSOURI RIVER. MAYOR ALBERT BEACH'S DAUGHTER, ELEANOR, POURED GRAPE JUICE ON THE PLANE'S NOSE.

For seven decades Gordon Parkinson wore the company color. Red hat, red sweater, red socks....

"These red pants are hard to find anymore," he said in a 1995 interview. "You see, I need another pair."

Parkinson was 87 then. His knees ached. His once-sparkling memories were fading from the effects of Alzheimer's disease. He was living out his retirement in a Kansas City home with red shutters, a red telephone and red Ford Taurus in the driveway.

Parkinson had been the operational planning manager and unofficial head cheerleader for the hometown airline when Trans World Airlines employed 10,000 people here. Most of those workers called him Parky. Or "Mr. TWA," as stitched on his red shirt.

Gone were the years when he gave speeches about TWA every week or two to local businesses and civic groups. On the day the retiree spoke with *The Kansas City Star*, he recalled in broad sweeps the decades past - from Lindbergh to TWA owner Howard Hughes to corporate raider Carl C. Icahn.

"It was a time," Mr. TWA said with a vague smile.

From a scrapbook Parkinson pulled a list of 200 co-workers from 1948. He had penciled 171 lines through those names, one for every worker who died.

Parkinson would die two years later. To many TWAers and all manner of industry analysts, the death of his old company was just a matter of time.

The carrier that ferried three popes and served the best chateaubriand in the sky seemed sadly out of step in Parky's final years. Twice in the 1990s TWA reorganized under federal bankruptcy protection. Upstart airlines, meantime, posted profits and packed in passengers by serving peanuts.

TWA from its earliest days had defied oddsmakers by pulling off financial loop-the-loops. Its spirit seemed as endless as the skies it traveled. But in time, so was its debt.

The airline's swashbucklers had long passed on.

Cancer killed Lindbergh in 1974. He offered early advice to TWA, when the letters meant Transcontinental and Western Air. He cast the swing vote that put its headquarters in Kansas City. He even let the airline promote itself as "The Lindbergh Line," though it really wasn't his.

Death came in 1976 to self-exiled TWA owner Howard Hughes, an orphan turned aviator turned troubled tycoon. A body once so elegant climbing out of cockpits had become "remarkably emaciated," an autopsy found.

A car wreck in 1959 claimed Jack Frye, a record-setting barnstormer who became TWA president at 30. He lived just long enough to forever change how the world flew.

TWA's trip rarely was smooth. Navigating through an industry in which straight years of profits were considered spectacular, its history is one of survival amid self-destructive egos.

In the 1930s the Kansas City-based airline lost millions of dollars and scores of lives to one day prove its doubters wrong. Two decades later, having flown soldiers to war and families to foreign lands, TWA faced ruin at the hands of Hughes - a stubborn genius losing his mind.

By 1970 it sailed the jet age "up, up and away," and Kansas City sailed with it. TWA bosses and workers alike made great wages, partied the holidays at the biggest company bash in town and flew free around the globe.

The airline sponsored Starlight Theater shows and other causes. It virtually defined the Northland, home to Parkinson and thousands of other TWAers who contributed heavily to Kansas City's tax base.

It was the first U.S. carrier to fly trans-continental and transatlantic at the same time, the first with in-flight movies, the first to offer domestic flights on the Boeing 747 jumbo jet.

Yes, Mr. TWA, it was a time.

"Oh, there was a tremendous amount of nostalgia for TWA," said former Vice Chairman Glenn Zander, somewhat sardonically, in the mid-1990s. "The premier airline with all these innovations. The airline of the stars. The best food...People didn't want it to change. And that still exists."

It existed - the nostalgia, the spirit, the hope - through the 20th century. But in the first month of the next century big news broke: American Airlines announced plans to acquire TWA in a surprise deal backed by both airlines. As TWA filed for Chapter 11 bankruptcy for the third time in a decade, its 3,500 workers in the Kansas City area moved closer to accepting the demise of their hometown airline.

More than seven decades after takeoff, a classic American company prepared for what looked to be its final approach. ✳

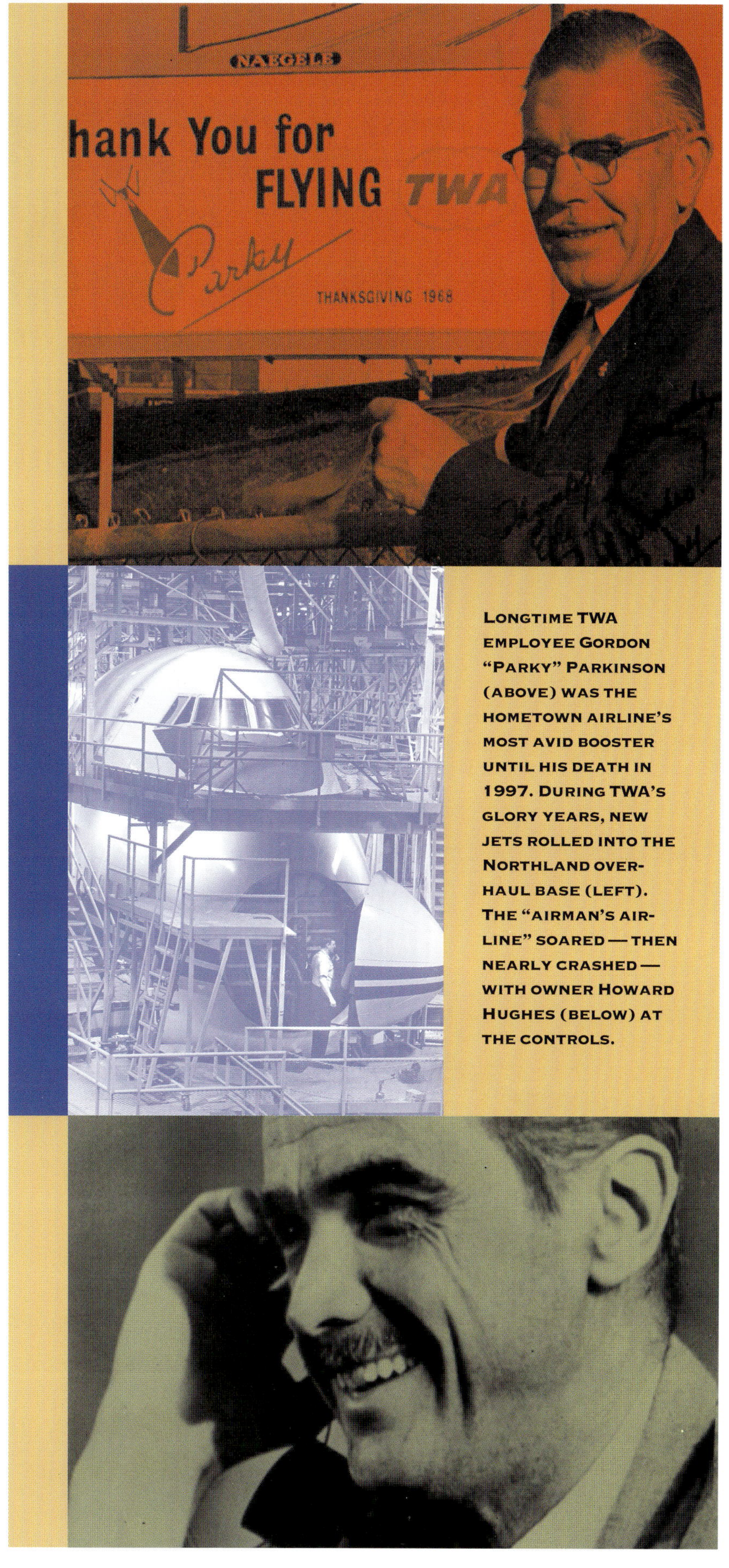

LONGTIME TWA EMPLOYEE GORDON "PARKY" PARKINSON (ABOVE) WAS THE HOMETOWN AIRLINE'S MOST AVID BOOSTER UNTIL HIS DEATH IN 1997. DURING TWA'S GLORY YEARS, NEW JETS ROLLED INTO THE NORTHLAND OVERHAUL BASE (LEFT). THE "AIRMAN'S AIRLINE" SOARED — THEN NEARLY CRASHED — WITH OWNER HOWARD HUGHES (BELOW) AT THE CONTROLS.

CHAPTER 1

THE AIRMAN'S AIRLINE

Trans World Airlines' history in Kansas City starts as it should, with personalities clashing. ✶ *"A man is a damn fool to get his feet off the ground," huffed City Manager Henry F. McElroy in the mid-1920s to Lou Holland, a stout Chamber of Commerce president. "Lou, let me tell you all there is to aviation. There's a lot of young bucks who learned to fly (during World War I). As soon as they have smashed the crates and killed themselves there will be no more flying."*

Holland had heard it before. In a railroad town hardly teeming with visionaries, he dared to look to the heavens as a way to broaden the industrial base. Friends who got rich from trains, grain and livestock called Holland "that nut on aviation."

Holland's pitch: "Air passenger lines? Do they mean anything to Kansas City? Does a duck swim?"

The politicians yawned.

Back then "passengers" meant thrill-seekers willing to wedge themselves in front of bouncing bags of airmail. Federal postal contracts sustained the few carriers that existed. But Holland, a photo engraver by trade, recognized that Kansas City sat in the center of a country poised to take flight.

It wasn't such a wild notion for someone who later invented a back-patting machine. "He never piloted an airplane," his son, Garratt Holland, recalled. "But he flew in one in Europe. It was fun, and Dad was fun-loving."

The first airmail chugged out of the Richards Flying Field near Swope Park on May 12, 1926. A year earlier, the Democratic cronies of political boss Tom Pendergast had taken over the City Council. When federal authorities declared Richards Field inadequate, Holland convinced McElroy and others in the Pendergast machine to build an airport near Downtown.

Then, in 1927, a St. Louis chum hooked Holland up with Charles Lindbergh, who had stunned the world by soaring solo across the Atlantic Ocean.

Lindbergh was an appealing superstar - humble and introspective, yet unmistakably daring, a prophet in racing goggles. The Little Falls, Minn., youth dropped out of college because he couldn't stick to the books. He

Transcontinental Air Transport's earliest tri-motor planes packed 10 passengers into wicker seats and flew below the clouds at 105 mph. Hailed "the father of Kansas City aviation," Lou Holland (right) lobbied in the 1920s for development of a Downtown airport. He also talked Charles Lindbergh (below) into paying a visit.

was an obscure airmail pilot when he began his historic flight to Paris on May 20, 1927. Thirty-four hours later he was the world's most celebrated airman.

Holland smelled a public-relations coup. Just three months after Lindbergh's flight, he convinced the ace to fly to Kansas City and dedicate an expanse of willows on the north bank of the Missouri River - soon to be known as Municipal Airport.

The city threw a parade. Throngs shouted "Lindy, Lindy, Lindy!" as a motorcade brought him from the airfield to Muehlebach Field on Brooklyn Avenue, where 10,000 spectators heard him speak. Even the naysaying city manager, McElroy, took his first plane ride that day, Aug. 17, which hap-pened to be McElroy's 62nd birthday. He proclaimed the flight "the greatest experience I ever had."

Lindbergh left satisfied, too. At a banquet he urged 500 civic leaders to court fledgling airlines and plane makers. "At present it may be doubtful in the minds of a number of Kansas City citizens as to whether the outlay required for this new airport was well spent or not," he said. "Within a few years, I do not believe there will be any doubt."

He promised big things for cities that took a chance on aviation, even if "we cannot foresee how many individuals will own a private plane 10 years from now."

So much couldn't be foreseen that night. The wily Holland, for one, had no clue that

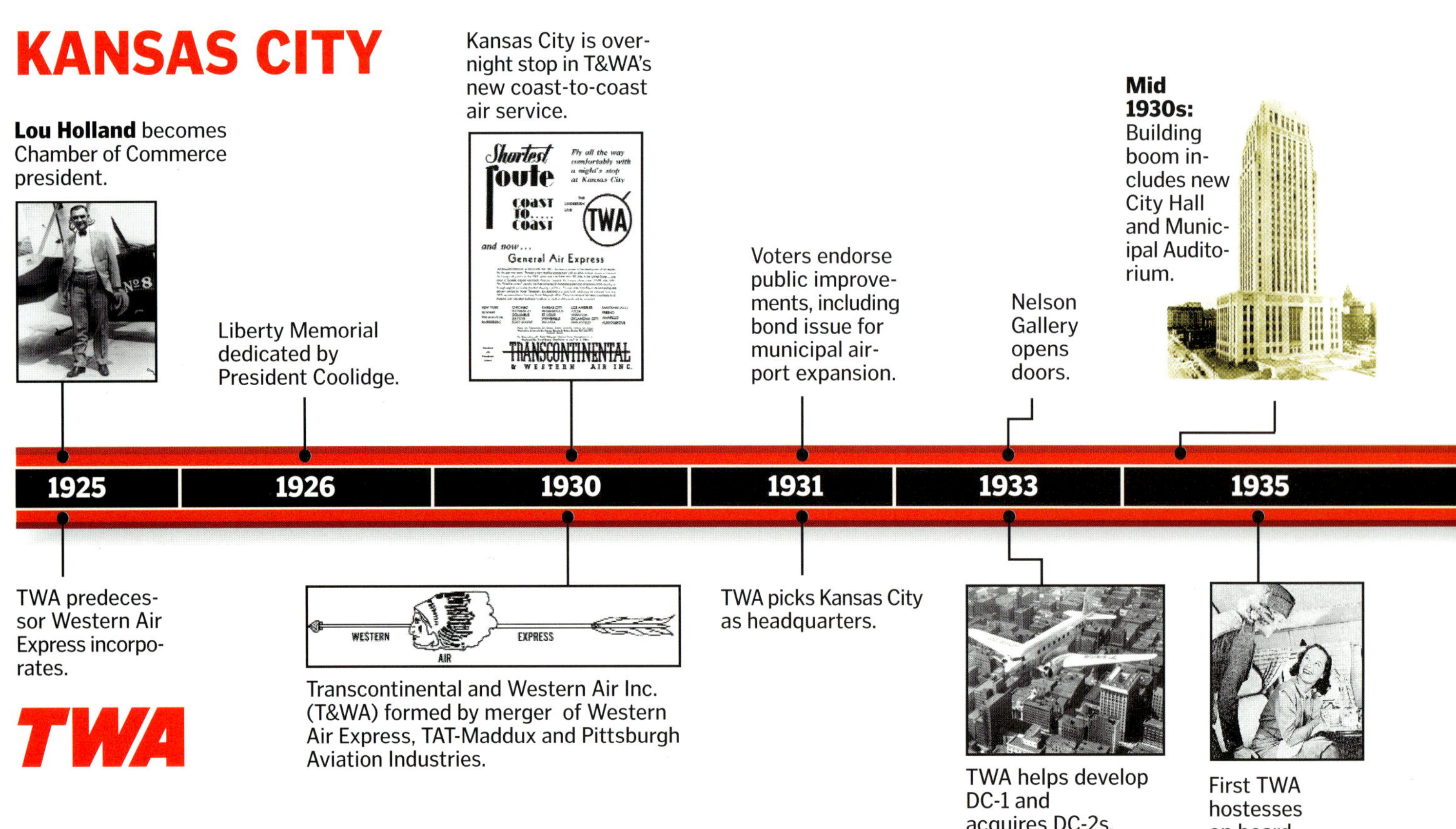

KANSAS CITY

Lou Holland becomes Chamber of Commerce president.

Liberty Memorial dedicated by President Coolidge.

Kansas City is overnight stop in T&WA's new coast-to-coast air service.

Voters endorse public improvements, including bond issue for municipal airport expansion.

Nelson Gallery opens doors.

Mid 1930s: Building boom includes new City Hall and Municipal Auditorium.

| 1925 | 1926 | 1930 | 1931 | 1933 | 1935 |

TWA predecessor Western Air Express incorporates.

TWA

Transcontinental and Western Air Inc. (T&WA) formed by merger of Western Air Express, TAT-Maddux and Pittsburgh Aviation Industries.

TWA picks Kansas City as headquarters.

TWA helps develop DC-1 and acquires DC-2s.

First TWA hostesses on board.

his guest of honor would someday work for an outfit destined to become Kansas City's airline.

Send - off by film stars

Transcontinental Air Transport lured Lindbergh into its lair with a $250,000 signing bonus, allowing the company to use his name for publicity. The fledgling airline also paid him $10,000 annually to chair its Technical Committee, a position he took to heart.

Lindbergh and his wife Anne toured all airfields on TAT's proposed cross-country route before declaring them suitable. Anne was stunned to discover on her visit to Kansas City that, despite the city's name, it was located in the state of Missouri.

On July 7, 1929, the legendary pilot pressed a ceremonial button in California, and Transcontinental Air Transport was wobbling skyward, cruising at 105 mph.

Silent-film stars Mary Pickford and Gloria Swanson christened the eastbound Ford Tri-Motors with magnums of grape juice, Prohibition-style. On the opposite coast, the famous Earhart climbed aboard a train en route for a plane for the westbound trip. One year after she became the first woman to fly across the Atlantic, her new mission was to be a relaxed passenger - elegantly attired in a polka-dotted dress - to promote flying to women travelers.

KANSAS CITY

Tom Pendergast
Tom Pendergast indicted; reform government sweeps out boss rule.

Tom Pendergast

Historic postcard of Downtown Airport
Expecting postwar boom, voters pass $41 million plan for roads and airport improvements.

Historic postcard of Downtown Airport

L. P. Cookingham is city manager; John B. Gage is mayor.

Harry Truman elected vice president, sworn in as president following April

Military leases Fairfax plant to TWA.

1939	1941	1944	1945	1947

Howard Hughes

Aviator Howard Hughes becomes principal stockholder.

TWA commits planes and pilots to war effort.

Record flight: Lockheed Constellation, Burbank to Washington, flown by Hughes and TWA president Jack Frye.

TWA awarded overseas routes.

Frye resigns as Hughes asserts power.

Jack Frye

Later-model Super G Constellation

TWA

CHARLES LINDBERGH

"I have felt the godlike power man derives from his machines ....the immortal viewpoint of higher air."

■ **BORN:** Feb. 4, 1902, in Detroit, Mich. The son of a U.S. congressman, Lindbergh spent most of his youth in Little Falls, Minn.

■ **EDUCATION:** His formal schooling ended during his sophomore year at the University of Wisconsin. He dropped out to attend a flying academy in Lincoln, Neb.

■ **PRIOR TO TWA:** As a pilot flying airmail between St. Louis and Chicago, he competed for a $25,000 prize offered to the first person to fly nonstop between New York and Paris. He made the flight in May 1927 in his monoplane, the Spirit of St. Louis.

■ **AT TWA:** He acted as technical advisor to the airline's predecessor, Transcontinental Air Transport, and mapped its first cross-country route in 1929. Two years later he served on Transcontinental & Western Air's site-selection committee, which picked Kansas City for its headquarters.

■ **DEPARTURE:** Following the kidnapping and murder of their 2-year-old son, Charles and Anne Morrow Lindbergh endured a sensational trial that led to the execution of Bruno Richard Hauptmann in 1936. The couple moved to Europe to escape publicity. After a tour of duty during World War II, the Lindberghs settled in Connecticut and he continued a business relationship with Pan American Airways. He died in Hawaii in 1974.

Kansas City's centrality had already shaped the city into a hub for railroads and trucking. But city leaders only vaguely appreciated at the time its position as the halfway point in coast-to-coast aviation.

The airline's first stop in Kansas City merited 10 paragraphs in *The Kansas City Times*. Bearing flowers, Lou Holland and a small band of local leaders greeted TAT general manager Paul Henderson. The newspaper reported that the group wished the airline success.

It lost $2.7 million in the next 18 months.

Financial distress, in fact, would help shape the airline into TWA. Having already merged with Maddux Air Lines, Transcontinental Air Transport merged again with the more profitable Western Air Express on Oct. 1, 1930. Airline historian Robert Serling called it "a shotgun marriage."

U.S. Postmaster General Walter Folger Brown, who issued airmail routes, ordered the wedding on the theory that the industry needed larger and fewer companies. His threat: No merger, no route.

Competing airlines cried fraud at the birth of Transcontinental & Western Air. But Kansas City lucked out. "T&WA" on Oct. 25, 1930, introduced all-air service from New York to Los Angeles - a 36-hour flight with one night's stop. And Kansas City's new airport blinked in the middle of the route.

That meant travelers spent the night at Downtown hotels.

Kansas City's location would soon pay off in other ways. Within a year TWA executives in New York decided to base its maintenance, ground operations and general offices in Kansas City, population 399,746.

"Kansas City lies ... within 12 hours flying time of any point on the company's system,"

After the 1930 merger that formed Transcontinental & Western Air, the airline for several years continued to rely on airmail contracts for the bulk of its revenues (above). TAT passengers received booklets (left) that charted the routes, listed the crew and included a "Certificate of Flight."

a TWA press release stated in 1931. It failed to mention that Kansas City chipped in $280,000 - about $3 million by today's standards - to help the cash-short airline build facilities.

TWA moved into a new building at 10 Richards Road on the airport grounds. The two-story headquarters and adjoining hangar reflected the times; the art-deco styling included an eagle figure, symbolizing flight, inlaid in the brick facade.

The city welcomed 250 new families and an annual $1 million in salaries. Nobody dreamed the payroll could swell past $25 million in two decades, although *The Kansas City Star* speculated:

"The importance of this gain to Kansas City is much greater than the immediate effect would indicate. ... There will be great centers of air service just as there are great railroad centers."

For that to happen, the airline needed to convince a rightfully skittish public that cruising through clouds wasn't foolish.

And that would take Jack Frye to help pull off.

Banking on bravado

A poker-playing pal named Harry Truman once said of Jack Frye: "He had imagination, which damn few businessmen have."

Imagination. Frye's business would crash without it.

Born William John Frye near Sweetwater, Okla., in 1904, he dropped out of high school at 17, spent a year in the Army Engineer Corps, then took jobs as a soda jerk, newspaper hawker and dishwasher in the Los Angeles area. He spent his modest earnings on

A SCRATCHY RECORDING

Historic Lindbergh speech delivered 250 employees, families to KC

If not for handsome hero Charles Lindbergh and round-faced "aviation nut" Lou Holland, TWA might have been the hometown airline of Tulsa, Okla.

Credit Kansas City's location, as many historians do, for the 1931 decision by Transcontinental & Western Air to land its headquarters here. Or credit Municipal Airport - blessed with public-funded improvements spearheaded by the political machine of Thomas J. Pendergast. The runways soon would hold enough Pendergast concrete to pave a 30-mile highway.

Those incentives certainly helped bring TWA to town. But so did a wax recording made four years earlier of Lindbergh speaking to local businessmen at a fancy dinner.

In August 1927, Holland headed the Chamber of Commerce. Lindbergh, fresh from his historic flight to Paris that spring, sat beside him at the Hotel President. The pilot had flown in to dedicate the new airfield Downtown.

After dining on stuffed lobster, Lindbergh stood before a roomful of civic types awed by his courage but skeptical about the future of flying. He spoke in a tight, low voice that later might be mistaken for actor Gary Cooper's.

"Any city which can obtain important airplane factories and transcontinental airlines will be benefited very greatly by them later on," he said. Jazzy, he wasn't. The audience sat on its hands for most of the lecture.

But Holland's ears perked up when Lindbergh suggested that Kansas City would someday make an ideal central headquarters for a coast-to-coast carrier.

The Airman's Airline

LOU HOLLAND'S TELEGRAM FROM NEW YORK HERALDED TWA'S DECISION IN 1931 TO BASE ITS HEADQUARTERS AT MUNICIPAL AIRPORT.

Little did Lindbergh know his speech was being broadcast and recorded a few miles away by a radio engineer named J.J. Warner.

And because no transcontinental service existed then, the aviator couldn't have known that by 1931 he'd be one of three members of a TWA committee selecting a home city.

Months before that committee's choice was made in New York, Holland gathered ammunition and went schmoozing. He placed ads in 105 newspapers promoting Kansas City as a place where "We Ride the Sky Lines!"

His contacts at the fledgling TWA were so chummy as to address Holland in memos as "My dear Lou." They informed him that Kansas City was among five sites under TWA's microscope. The others: Tulsa (favored by Oklahoma native and TWA vice president Jack Frye); Amarillo, Texas; Wichita and Lindbergh's preference, St. Louis.

Holland invited Lindbergh to Kansas City six weeks before the committee was to decide. "I have a lodge on a lake," Holland wrote, "and am sure you would have an enjoyable time."

Lindbergh declined. But the third committee member, J.L. Maddux, toured Kansas City in the spring of 1931 and flew away impressed. Holland had scheduled Maddux's visit on what was hailed as Kansas City Day. The citywide rally was scripted to celebrate the passage of a $40 million public improvements package called the 10-Year Plan.

Maddux told the local press: "It's the most remarkable thing I ever heard of. With the remainder of the country complaining about hard times, Kansas City puts over this great program."

With Maddux sold, Holland focused on committee member Frye, who favored Tulsa. Holland compiled a notebook that compared Kansas City's transportation trade to Tulsa's. Then he swayed the City Council to draft an incentive package to match Tulsa's.

As for swaying Lindbergh, Holland produced a secret weapon: The wax recording from 1927.

The phonograph disc of Lindbergh's speech at the Hotel President would be saved for posterity. Part of it today is a scratchy mess. That's because Holland took the record to New York and played Lindbergh's glowing remarks about Kansas City over and over for the committee's consideration, according to his son, Garratt Holland.

The ploy worked. Lindbergh cast the swing vote for Kansas City, 2-1 over Tulsa.

Holland wired home on June 16, 1931:

"Tomorrows papers will carry story. Transcontinental Line selected Kansas City headquarters. Have had quite a battle since Sunday but won….Two hundred fifty employees and familys (sic)…Big victory Kansas City."

Chamber President Conrad Mann wrote back: "To you and you alone goes the credit for this accomplishment."

flying lessons.

At age 20 he borrowed money from his brother to invest in the Burdett Flying School of California, where Frye began teaching. Soon, he and two associates bought out the school's owner. The renamed Aero Corp. rapidly expanded into all areas of aviation service: movie stunt flying, charter flights, aircraft maintenance, passenger express routes.

Frye's ambition soared along. He was only 26 when he became the first vice president of operations for the merged TWA, prompting his eventual move to Kansas City.

At the time flying was 1,500 times more deadly than riding on trains.

Such dangers just added weight to the industry's load of public-relations problems. Passengers paid handsomely to get sick in flight. Inside a cabin crammed with wicker seats, their conversations competed with the din of engines. Chit-chat was out of the question with windows opened for ventilation.

Rough weather rendered some flights so unbearable that entire cabins were hosed out afterward. TWA employees spoke of "the vomit comet to Albuquerque" only half-jokingly.

The adventure appealed mostly to society wags and celebrities looking for publicity. Frye eagerly obliged. Phone calls and telegrams to newspapers, alerting them to a movie star landing at the nearest airport, became a daily practice of TWA's marketing crew.

"It was bravado," said Serling, author of *Howard Hughes' Airline: An Informal History of TWA*, in a 1994 interview. "If you told someone, 'I just flew from Washington to Kansas City,' it was like saying you went three rounds with Jack Dempsey."

On the slowest days the airline planted shills - employees who were supposed to look like customers - "just to give the passengers some company," said retired pilot Ed Betts.

TWA's advertisements stressed safety and glamour at Frye's insistence. He backed it up with awesome derring-do behind the scenes, sending TWA researcher Tommy Tomlinson 20,000 feet into the air with an oxygen mask to test the viability of flying above bad weather.

Frye favored fat cigars, fast cars, pretty women and natty clothes - an airman's airman. Four times he married, the last to a Las Vegas showgirl. Like the Kansas City jazz age in which he lived, he was far more forward-thinking than his loose posture and devil-may-care persona suggested.

Once his pilots insisted they couldn't make all of their scheduled stops, so he hopped in a plane and did it himself, setting a transcontinental speed record.

"He was a practical dreamer," said historian Serling.

ONE-TIME BARNSTORMER
JACK FRYE (RIGHT)
BECAME TWA PRESIDENT
IN 1934 AT AGE 30.
HE PUSHED FOR THE DE-
VELOPMENT OF SAFER,
FASTER PLANES SUCH AS
THE DC-2. (BELOW AND
RIGHT) A BROCHURE AND
PROMOTIONAL PHOTO
SHOW WELL-DRESSED
PASSENGERS BOARDING
AND DEPARTING. BY
THE 1950S THEY FELT
SAFE ENOUGH TO BRING
THEIR CHILDREN.

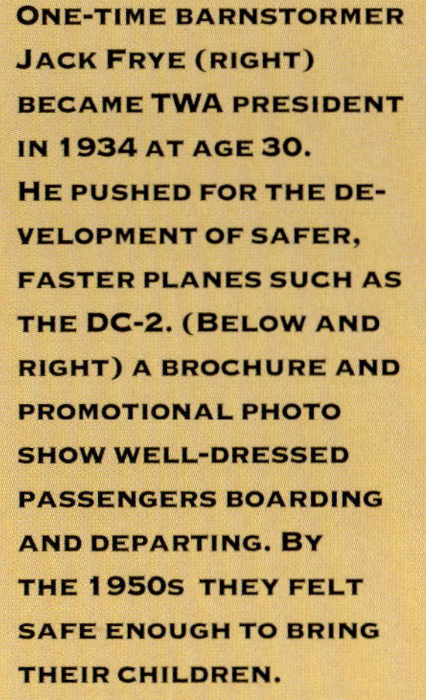

TRANSCONTINENTAL
& WESTERN AIR, INC.
TWA
FASTEST COAST TO COAST

TWA
35 • THE • LINDBERGH • LINE

TWA
TWA

WILLIAM JOHN "JACK" FRYE

"That plane (the Constellation) really can take it."

- ■ **BORN:** March 18, 1904, near Sweetwater, Okla. Only 8 when his mother died, he was raised by his father and grandparents on a ranch in Wheeler, Texas.

- ■ **EDUCATION:** He dropped out of high school at 17 and spent a year in the Army Engineer Corps.

- ■ **PRIOR TO TWA:** As part owner of the Aero Corporation of California, he headed a subsidiary, Standard Air Lines, that introduced passenger service between Los Angeles and Tucson, Ariz., via Phoenix. Standard in 1929 became the western link in a cross-country route combining air and rail service. The company was sold a year later to Western Air Express, which soon merged with Transcontinental Air Transport to form TWA.

- ■ **AT TWA:** As vice president of operations in 1930, he developed the nation's first all-air service from coast to coast, a 36-hour trip with an overnight stop in Kansas City. He became TWA president, based in Kansas City, in 1934. Frye's vision led to development of the Douglas DC-2. He secured financial backing from Howard Hughes to allow TWA to acquire the Boeing 307 Stratoliner and Lockheed Constellation, which the airline used to inaugurate international passenger service in 1946.

- ■ **DEPARTURE:** A hated rival of Hughes assistant Noah Dietrich, Frye resigned in 1947 after failing to produce profits. He became president of the General Aniline and Film Corp. in New York, which he left in 1955 to form his own aeronautics company. He died in a car wreck in 1959.

Perilous to prestigious

Les Munger flew for TWA then. He knew how impractical it was.

"There were days when we couldn't fly because we didn't have enough money to buy gasoline," said Munger, who by the 1990s had retired to Johnson County. "I had the idea that flying might get better but never too great."

Hollywood types boarded because they loved being photographed at airports, where sightseers often camped. "Movie people were our chief source of passengers," Munger said. "Jimmy Stewart, nice fella."

Parky Parkinson was a TWA meteorologist then.

Fog and wind spelled death, he knew. Early pilots had to see the ground to know where to go. Beacons five to 10 miles apart directed them to the next city. From the ground Parkinson checked air currents: "You'd float up a balloon and see how fast it went."

What seems by today's standards a rickety way to travel was actually prestigious by the mid-1930s. Five-course steak meals and cherry pie for dessert were provided by the trendy Fred Harvey Restaurant chain. Co-pilots served coffee provided they gargled first in the cockpit.

"Air hostesses" boarded in 1935.

Two thousand women applied for the first training session in Kansas City; 30 were selected. All had to be registered nurses, Frye's way of instilling a sense of safety. Those with big feet were urged in company letters to reconsider their applications. Married women needn't apply, either.

Ruth Rhodes Molitor left her nursing job in Philadelphia to become TWA's first chief

TWA IN THE 1930S AND '40S PROMOTED SAFETY AND ATTENTIVE, LUXURIOUS SERVICE TO PURSUADE AMERICANS TO TAKE FLIGHT. THE AIRLINE PUSHED FOR THE DEVELOPMENT OF ALL-METAL AIRCRAFT TO REPLACE RISKY WOODEN PLANES, AND TWA TAPPED REGISTERED NURSES TO BE HOSTESSES. RUTH RHODES (UPPER LEFT) WAS TWA'S FIRST CHIEF HOSTESS.

TWA Airline Hostess

TWA Color-foto

hostess. She chose TWA because of its motto, "The Lindbergh Line." And while training in Kansas City, she learned the airline's definition of "ladylike."

Using your fingers to whistle for a taxi was not ladylike. One TWA hostess was fired for doing it.

"We knew all the passengers' names then," said Molitor, now living in Franklin, Tennessee. "We offered chewing gum for when their ears popped. We pointed out landmarks. Oh, it was delightful."

John Roche became a TWA engineer about the time Frye's airline introduced the DC-3 in 1937. With room for up to 28 people, it was the first plane big enough to allow a carrier to profit off passengers instead of mail.

Roche and his drafting mates got assignments to improve aircraft every week: An air-conditioning hatch. A music system. A tank for de-icing propellers.

"The question, 'Is this possible?' was interesting to someone like Jack Frye," Roche recalled six decades later. "Technology really made huge steps in a short period."

Hughes on board

All of the glitz and innovations couldn't lift red ink off the balance sheet. In its first three years, Transcontinental & Western Air posted losses totaling $1.2 million. Nobody's salary exceeded $20,000, nobody had received a bonus and no stockholder saw a dividend check.

In 1934 a memo out of Kansas City informed that "the entire personnel of T&WA is furloughed." The federal government had just canceled airmail contracts, shifting that job to the Army. The action triggered a

ROCKNE'S DEATH

Shocking air crash becomes a public-relations horror

Bound for Hollywood to make a football movie, Notre Dame coach Knute Rockne lumbered aboard a TWA plane in Kansas City on the morning of March 31, 1931.

Eighty minutes into the flight, a storm hit and the right wing snapped off. The Fokker F-10 spiraled into a Kansas pasture, killing the beloved coach and seven others on board. An investigation pointed to the simplest of hazards - wood rot and ice - underscoring how much the industry needed to learn.

The early years of commercial aviation were unspeakably ugly. More than a few boarding passengers stepped into spinning propellers. Once off the ground, a 1930 traveler's chance of dying was 1,500 times greater than it was on trains, according to aviation historian Robert Serling.

TWA in its infancy played a key role in advancing airline safety. It had to, if TWA was going to lure wary Americans to the skies.

The Rockne crash was a public-relations horror. One of the most famous sports figures in the country at the time of his death, the 43-year-old native Norwegian had wrapped up two undefeated seasons leading Notre Dame's Fighting Irish. Ten thousand fans jammed a Chicago train station when his casket rolled through. Millions wordwide tuned their radios for the live broadcast of his funeral. Kansas Citians wept for two of Rockne's sons, who attended the Pembroke School for Boys.

Reporters demanded to know how a wing could drop off a plane less than 18 months old. Government rules would soon turn wooden aircraft into scrap.

But the most dramatic reaction came from the airline.

From his Kansas City office TWA executive Jack Frye dispatched a single page of specifications for a metal ship that would reinvent travel. Douglas Aircraft Co. was the only manufacturer to take him up. Frye wrote that the plane must "make satisfactory take-offs under good control at any TWA airport" - with one of its two engines out.

They named it

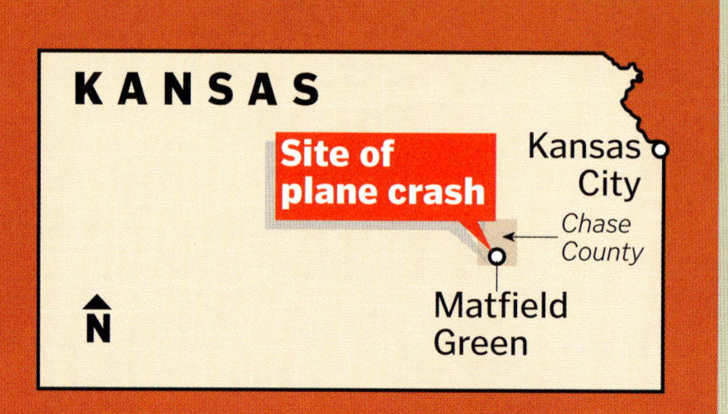

DC-1.

Such advancements didn't make TWA immune from tragedies that the company later chalked up as "growing pains." Among them:

■ In May 1935, U.S. Sen. Bronson Cutting of New Mexico occupied Seat 11 inside a TWA DC-2 running out of fuel. The pilot, unable to land in Kansas City because of fog, headed for an emergency field in Kirksville, Mo. He strayed off course, sank too low and struck an embankment. Four passengers and both pilots were killed, but it was Cutting's death that sounded alarms in Washington.

So came the Civil Aeronautics Act. It created an independent board to probe air accidents.

■ Ten persons died in 1936 when a TWA plane crashed into a snowy Pennsylvania hillside. The flight "hostess," Nellie Granger of Kansas City, trudged more than 4 miles in the cold to flag down a car. Despite her cuts and bruises, she insisted upon returning with rescue crews to help survivors. Even *The New York Times* hailed the "plucky heroine."

Only months earlier TWA had reluctantly hired hostesses. Granger's feat confirmed their worth and lent credence to the airline's policy that they be trained nurses.

■ Actress Carole Lombard died when a DC-3 slammed into a mountain east of Los Angeles in 1942.

The air safety board blamed a TWA captain "who insisted on flying as if radio had never been invented," wrote aviation author Carl Solberg. Other TWA crews suspected the pilot was chatting with Lombard, Clark Gable's wife, when the plane crashed.

■ After a 1946 wreck, federal regulators temporarily grounded the Constellation - the state-of-the-art plane that promised to carry TWA into globe-girdling glory.

The accident killed five airmen, and the grounding cost TWA millions. It had just gone international and needed to expand domestic routes after the war.

"I wish I had a dollar for everyone who's said the industry isn't as good as it used to be," writer Serling told *The Kansas City Star* a half-century later. "What I remember is covering too many crashes."

scathing telegram to President Franklin D. Roosevelt from Lindbergh. Within four months - and after the deaths of several Army pilots - the government reversed course and TWA was back to flying the mail.

Always hunting for capital, Frye in 1938

wanted a $15 million infusion for bigger airplanes that could fly higher and faster than any before.

TWA's investors in New York balked. So he sought out a kindred spirit, another airman with the deepest of pockets.

Howard R. Hughes had just made headlines flying a self-modified plane around the world in three days, 19 hours when Frye approached him for money.

"Good God, Jack," Hughes said. "Don't you realize that's a small fortune?"

At least the dashing heir to the Hughes Tool Co. fortune thought $15 million small. And by the spring of 1939, Hughes had bought out TWA's major stockholders. He was 33, younger even than Frye.

The airline would eventually become the Texas tycoon's favorite toy, obsessing Hughes far more than oil drilling or movie making. He never held a position at TWA. But his influence would shape it for better or worse for decades.

His early investments clearly helped TWA set new standards. The pressurized Boeing Stratoliner, introduced in 1940, was the first airliner to lift passengers to altitudes where oxygen runs out, above rough weather.

Stratoliners proved vital when World War II broke. TWA agreed to race its own planes and pilots overseas, hauling cargo one way and wounded soldiers the other.

But Hughes' crowning achievement came in 1944 with the unveiling of the Lockheed Constellation. With the three-tailed "Connie," Hughes' money and technical wizardry blended perfectly with Frye's flair for public relations - a talent Hughes never had nor understood.

Hughes and Frye introduced the Connie by strapping themselves in the cockpit in Burbank, Calif., and setting a seven-hour speed record to Washington, where they turned the sleek ship over to the Army Air Force. The media ate it up, although military dignitaries were less than pleased that the plane touted TWA's logo and flashy red stripes.

The airline would go through 147 Connies in the next 20 years.

Roomy enough to let you rise from your seat without wrenching your back, it was the first passenger plane to cruise at 300 mph. It remained a favorite among TWA retirees, 200 of whom danced in Kansas City at the plane's 50th birthday party.

The Connie promised to be TWA's ticket to worldwide glory. When World War II ended, the airline was the first in the United States to fly both domestic and transatlantic routes. The future should have seemed brighter than ever.

There was just one problem: TWA still was spending more money than it was bringing in.

Moneyman Hughes and his closest adviser, Noah Dietrich, grew restless with president Frye. A pilots' strike cost the airline an estimated $7 million. A Connie crash and a peacetime demand for more routes tightened the vise.

TWA lost $8.9 million in 1946, despite flying passengers all the way to Shanghai and becoming the world-class carrier Frye always knew it could be. Under pressure from Hughes, Frye resigned in 1947.

He would be the first of a long series of executives who were fired, quit, or in one case, died of a heart attack as the unpredictable Hughes asserted power.

Frye was largely forgotten in the postwar bustle, though he managed to land executive posts at smaller companies paying four times his top salary at TWA. He left his Kansas City home for Arizona, where he tried to develop a short-haul aircraft for underdeveloped countries. It died on the drawing board.

On Feb. 3, 1959, a drunken driver in Tucson struck Frye's sports car broadside, killing the man credited for making air travel safer.

By coincidence, it happened on a road outside Hughes' plane factory. ✳

A FINANCIAL INFUSION BY HOWARD HUGHES (ABOVE) HELPED TWA REVOLUTIONIZE PASSENGER SERVICE. AS WORLD WAR II LOOMED, ARTIST GEORGE PETTY SKETCHED THE PATRIOTIC TWA HOSTESS (LEFT). A TWA POSTCARD BELOW TOUTS THE PRESSURIZED STRATOLINER, INTRODUCED IN 1940.

CHAPTER 2

HUGHES' STORMY REIGN

Howard Hughes swaggers into a cockpit crammed with newspaper writers to show off his latest gadget. The mission is "to crash or not to crash," quips Hughes, who at 41 casually refers to TWA as "my airline." ✴ He eases the TWA Constellation skyward. He races to the Topa Topa Mountains, a West Coast graveyard for reckless pilots. A mile-high cliff looms ahead as Hughes speeds closer. ✴ Closer. Reporters squirm. Some wonder if the reclusive tycoon really is unstable. In 10 seconds the plane will hit the mountain at 225 mph. ✴ Suddenly, amber lights blink near Hughes' seat. A bell sounds. Hughes yanks the wheel hard and dodges the cliff. ✴ He declares what is now obvious: The new radar works.

As gray-flannel business types took over other air carriers, Trans World Airlines was ruled in the 1940s and '50s by a stubble-faced aviator who dressed so shabbily he got the bum's rush when he tried to get inside the Hotel Muehlebach.

Howard Hughes held most of TWA's stock but no official position, nor did he visit the Kansas City headquarters often. But he was one remarkable airman. And during his turbulent reign - one of grand achievements and nearly disastrous power trips - TWA billed itself "the Airman's Airline."

And, as with his daredevil demonstration near the Topa Topa Mountains in 1947, Hughes would put TWA itself on a crash course during the next 14 years. Eventually, the airman's airline would buckle under the weight of the airman's ego.

Hughes hired and fired presidents in rapid succession. While other airlines embraced speedy "jets" over piston planes, he delayed TWA's entry into the jet age.

Seven years of profit in the 1950s, when TWA built its state-of-the-art overhaul base in the Northland of Kansas City, were followed by three straight losses.

Hughes finally hatched a scheme for TWA to lease jets from his own Hughes Tool Co. and thereby lower his taxes. But by 1960, the demand for jet travel would force him to

FLYING A CONSTELLA-
TION, HOWARD HUGHES
DEMONSTRATED A NEW
RADAR WARNING
SYSTEM TO THE PRESS
IN APRIL 1947. THE
TECHNICAL BRILLIANCE
OF TWA'S MAJOR STOCK-
HOLDER WOULD SOON
BE OVERSHADOWED BY
HIS BIZARRE MANNER
OF DOING BUSINESS AND
A STUBBORN REFUSAL
TO GIVE IN TO WALL
STREET.

seek financing from the big-time lenders he despised.

The lenders eventually would oust Hughes and turn TWA into Wall Street's airline.

Much has been spoken and written of the billionaire Hughes, who died a scruffy recluse in 1976. But the most concise description may have come from his own lips before his slide into dementia.

"I suppose," he said in a 1948 interview, "I'm not like other men."

Brilliant, kind, mysterious

Howard Robard Hughes Jr. was a Texan, the only son of the man whose rock-drill bit revolutionized the oil industry. His mother constantly fretted over young Howard's health, a preoccupation that troubled Hughes in later years.

The boy had difficulty making friends but had a knack for things mechanical. One of his earliest creations was a radio he made out of doorbell parts.

Both of his parents died before Hughes was 18. In a characteristic show of independence, he defied the wishes of relatives by quitting school and seizing control of the Hughes Tool Co.

But he was not content to be a millionaire in the oil industry. He made movies in Hollywood and squired around town with starlets such as Jean Harlow, a Kansas City native. He set aviation records and formed Hughes

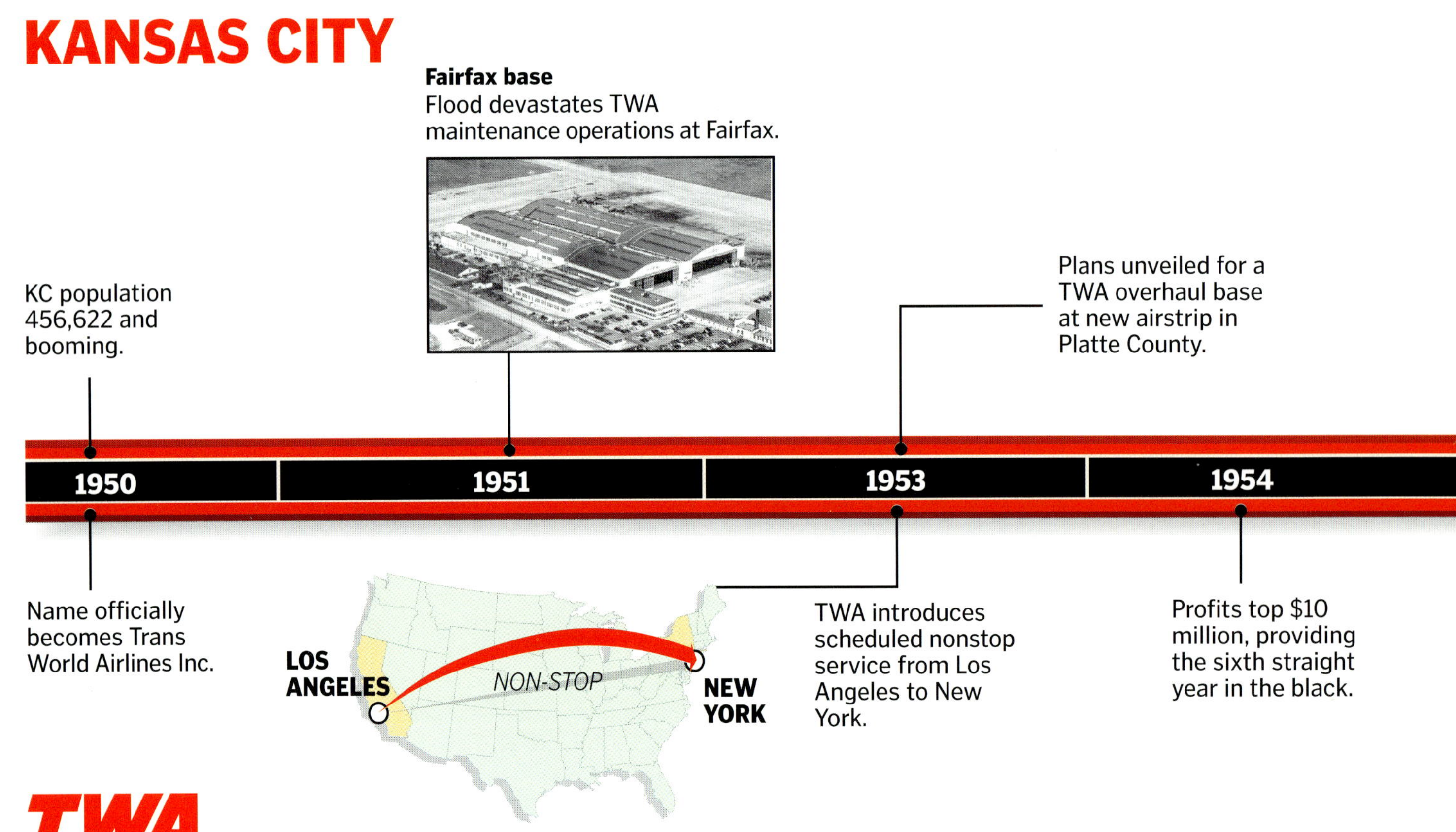

Hughes' Stormy Reign

Aircraft Co., which became one of the nation's biggest defense contractors.

Hughes began buying TWA stock in 1939, the result of company president Jack Frye's hunting for someone to finance a new fleet of planes.

"Guess which one is Howard Hughes," Frye would playfully tell visitors to his Kansas City office whenever Hughes was to drop in. "Bet you can't."

Frye usually won the bet. "That was Hughes?" the uninitiated would say.

Despite his baggy pants, tossed hair and open collar, Hughes won deep respect from TWA's rank-and-file because he designed aircraft - albeit some as far-fetched as the mammoth "Spruce Goose," a flying plywood boat built with military money. It flew once for about a mile.

Avery Dickson, a retired TWA mechanic who lives in Raymore, remembered seeing Hughes when he visited the TWA overhaul shop at Kansas City's old Municipal Airport.

"When he came up to a man to talk to him, he put his hand out, and you'd better shake hands with him whether your hand was greasy or not," said Dickson, who never got to talk to Hughes. "And if he got grease on his hand, you just gave him a rag and he wiped it off just like he worked there with you."

Hughes could be kind. He once dispatched a plane to get an iron lung for the polio-stricken daughter of an acquaintance. He could be brilliant. In the mid-1940s, he

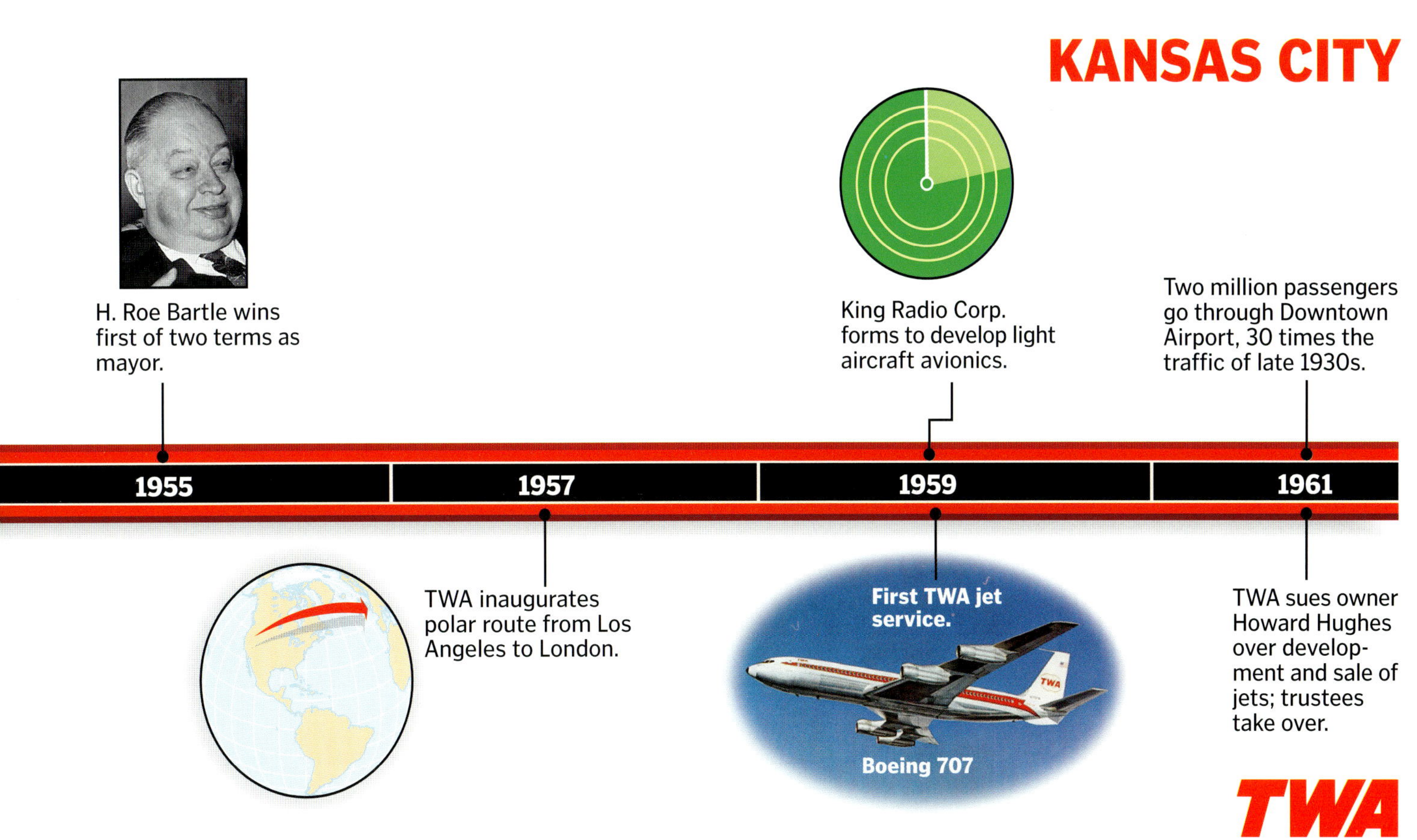

helped conceive the Lockheed Constellation, the fastest and most advanced passenger plane of its time.

But always he was mysterious.

The "Connie" project exemplified his obsession with secrecy. Hughes and TWA president Frye visited Lockheed's plant incognito, wearing fake employee badges to check out the work.

Hughes' code name for Frye was "Jesus Christ." The mogul called himself "God."

Hughes once said: "I'm not nearly as interested in people as I should be, I guess. What I am tremendously interested in is science, nature and its various manifestations, the Earth and the minerals that come out of it."

When Hughes would stay at the palatial Hotel Muehlebach in Downtown Kansas City, "he was nothing special," recalled Philip Pistilli, chairman of the Raphael Hotel Group and former Muehlebach manager, in 1995. "He was just another business executive. A good guest."

But a Muehlebach doorman named Charlie held another opinion in 1945.

Hughes strolled up to Charlie sporting stubble, a soiled shirt, dirty tennis shoes and trousers held up by a rope, former *Kansas City Star* aviation editor Justin Bowersock recalled years later.

"Where do you think you are going?" the doorman demanded to know.

"To my suite in this hotel," replied Hughes.

"Oh yeah? Get on your way," Charlie barked.

"But I'm Howard Hughes, and I have the presidential suite."

The doubtful doorman checked inside the hotel to make sure. Seconds later he popped back out and said, "Yes sir, Mr. Hughes. May I escort you to the elevator?"

Growth after war

TWA truly was the airman's airline when World War II ended. Run by money man Hughes and president Frye, himself a record-setting pilot, it spread out in a hurry to provide unprecedented global connections for peacetime travelers.

When Charles Smirl joined the local headquarters in 1946, "we didn't know it was going to pick up like it did. A lot of us who got connected with flying in the war just wanted to stay in that business. It got into our blood."

Yet 1946 proved to be a watershed year for TWA. Having mastered the ferrying of cargo during the war, the airline revved up for passenger service overseas.

In the next five years TWA became the first airline to provide all-cargo service across the Atlantic and the first with all-sleeper luxury service on its international "Sky Chief."

But pioneering was pricey. Though revenues were way up, the airline lost $15 mil-

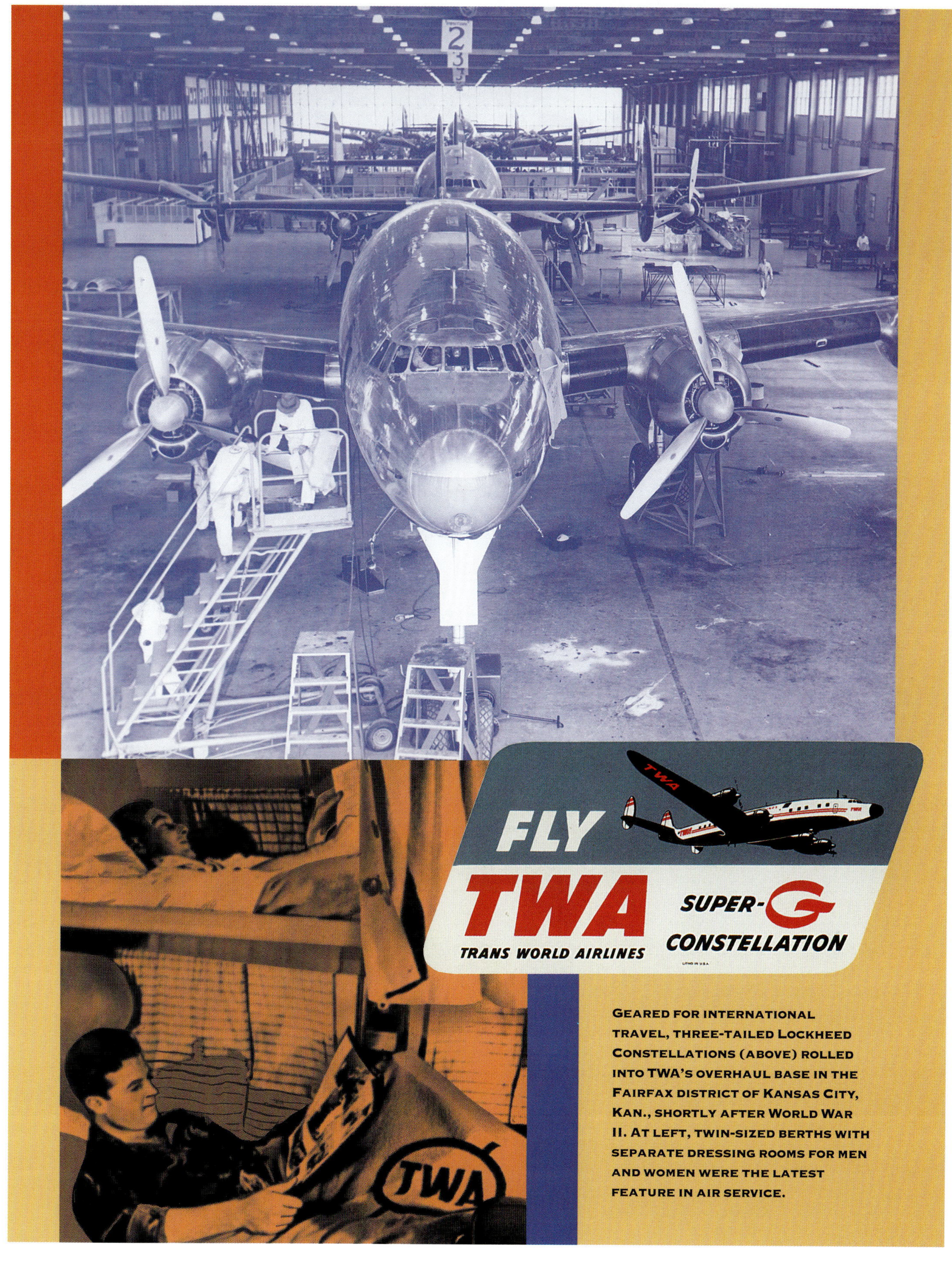

Geared for international travel, three-tailed Lockheed Constellations (above) rolled into TWA's overhaul base in the Fairfax district of Kansas City, Kan., shortly after World War II. At left, twin-sized berths with separate dressing rooms for men and women were the latest feature in air service.

HOWARD ROBARD HUGHES

*"I have never liked this plan
(to surrender control of TWA).
I assure you that if it is employed
it will be over my dead body."*

■ **BORN:** Although no birth certificate has survived, his aunt signed an affidavit placing Hughes' birth on Christmas Eve, 1905, in Houston, Texas.

■ **EDUCATION:** He studied at the California Institute of Technology despite having no high-school diploma. He later enrolled at Rice Institute of Technology but dropped out, following his father's death, to take over the Hughes Tool Co.

■ **PRIOR TO TWA:** He moved to Hollywood in 1926 to produce films such as "Hell's Angels" and "Scarface." Hughes also founded an aircraft company and, in 1935, set a world speed record in a plane of his own design.

■ **AT TWA:** In 1939, as he and TWA president Jack Frye conceived plans for larger aircraft, Hughes began acquiring stock. He owned 45 percent and a controlling interest of TWA within five years; by 1960 he held 78 percent of its outstanding stock. His money and technical enterprise helped the airline become a global carrier on the wings of the Lockheed Constellation. In the 1950s he retreated from public view and developed increasingly hostile relations with a string of TWA executives.

■ **DEPARTURE:** Reluctant to buy jets, Hughes steered TWA into red ink in the late 1950s. Lenders in 1960 forced him to relinquish control and put his TWA stock into a voting trust. Forever pining to reclaim TWA, the shriveled recluse died in 1976 on a plane racing to take him to a Texas hospital.

lion between 1946 and 1948, partly because of a pilots' strike. The losses annoyed Hughes and forced the exits of Frye and Frye's successor, LaMotte Cohu.

In came Ralph S. Damon, a one-time pilot and former American Airlines president. Well liked by his subordinates, Damon pitched the airman's airline concept and encouraged workers to stay upbeat.

"I've been thinking," Damon once told a colleague over coffee at the Hotel President. "If we could get everyone telling positive stories, we could have a great part in turning the economy around!"

TWA finished the '40s in the black - thanks in large part to Damon's cost-cutting moves, such as shutting down an international maintenance base in Delaware and consolidating all overhaul operations in Kansas City. The overhaul base in the Fairfax district had 4,158 workers on a $23 million payroll.

By then the airline had instilled undying devotion in local TWA workers such as the late Ray Dunn. He arose in the Hughes era from mechanic to senior executive.

"It was a different time in the American workplace," said his son, Tom Dunn. "Dad would go into the hangar and know everyone's job. He'd be on the phone at 2 a.m. talking to Rome about aircraft. In periods of strike, he'd go out to that overhaul base to keep it going."

Ray Dunn was the first to inspect the wreckage at the Fairfax overhaul base from Kansas City's 1951 flood.

Rowing in oily currents that had swallowed TWA 's Fairfax hangars, his oar rings wrapped in cloth to prevent sparks, he found six aircraft and countless spare parts under 15 feet of water.

The flood "wiped us out," he later told au-

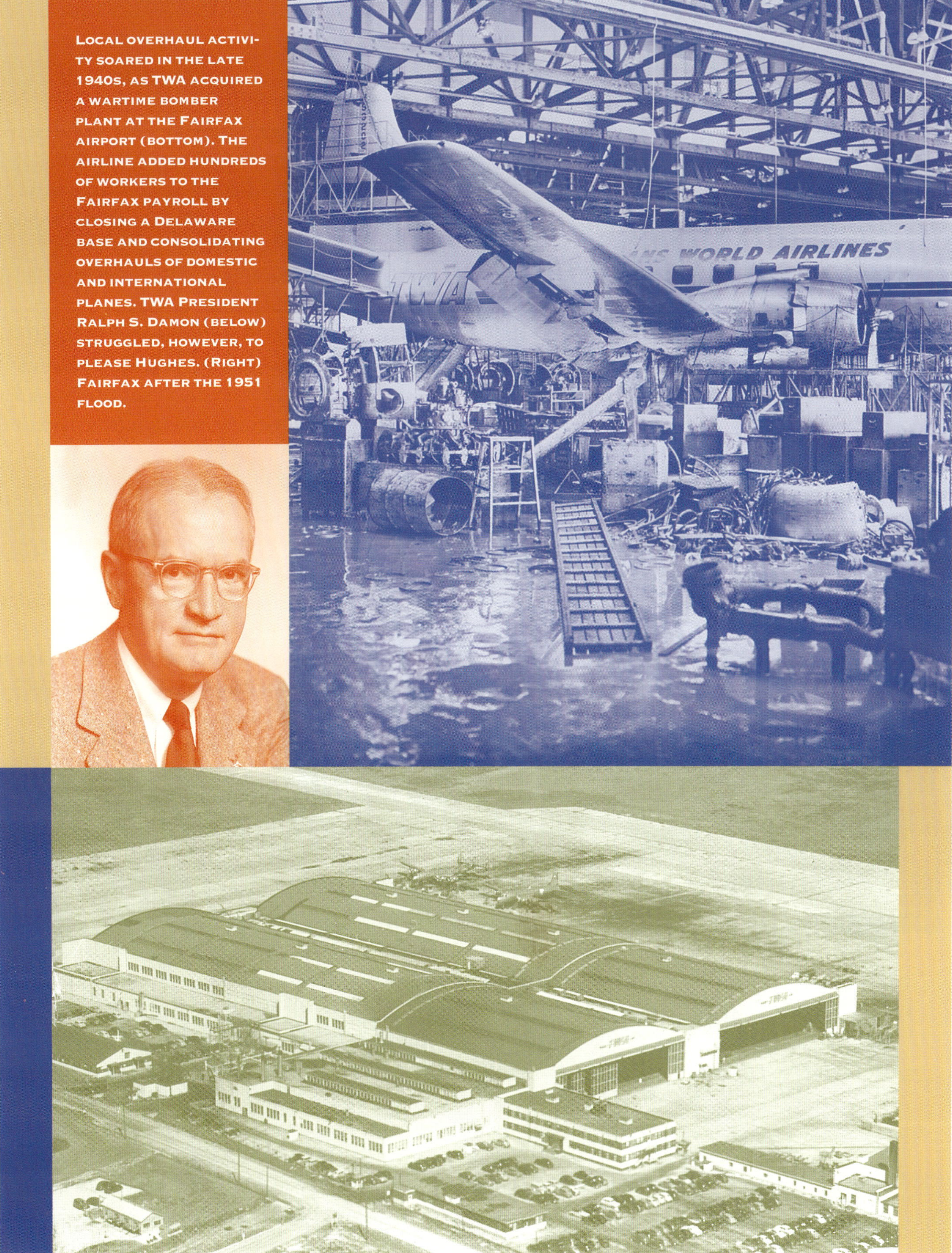

Local overhaul activity soared in the late 1940s, as TWA acquired a wartime bomber plant at the Fairfax airport (bottom). The airline added hundreds of workers to the Fairfax payroll by closing a Delaware base and consolidating overhauls of domestic and international planes. TWA President Ralph S. Damon (below) struggled, however, to please Hughes. (Right) Fairfax after the 1951 flood.

thor and former TWA executive Robert Rummel. "It was only through the dedication of the good working people at the base that we managed to keep the airline flying."

John Collings was another company lifer whose employment dated to Day One - as a pilot for the TWA's predecessor, Transcontinental Air Transport, in 1929. By the early 1950s he was an executive vice president, lobbying the city hard to help the airline build an overhaul base on high ground, near a proposed 7,300-foot runway.

The open space 18 miles north of Downtown would allow pilots to ease a big plane down without the white-knuckle landings that made tiny Municipal Airport infamous among airmen.

TWA enjoyed an unusual string of profits through 1955 as more Americans took to the skies.

Because of Hughes' Hollywood ties, TWA planes also appeared in more movies than any airline of the era. "One of my jobs," recalled former TWA publicist Larry Hilliard, "was to assign photos of Debbie Reynolds or David Niven boarding a TWA flight and servicing the newspapers.

"Cary Grant was one of the few close friends of Howard Hughes," Hilliard said. That explains why a TWA airliner was shown behind Grant's shoulder, with no apparent relevance, in the 1959 thriller "North by Northwest."

Hughes resisted jets

Travelers in the mid-1950s began sneaking peaks at a new kind of flying: Passenger jets - twice as fast as piston aircraft - were quickly becoming the industry rage.

And soon the world learned what could go wrong in an airman's airline.

The airman in Hughes was fascinated by jet technology. But the inventor in him was jealous that others had thought of it first. So as the rest of the industry raced to place orders with established jet makers, Hughes dawdled in the hope that his airline would someday fly jets with his own personal touches - just as it did with the piston-powered Connie.

He pursued a fuzzy dream of designing his own jets while TWA's competitors lined up Boeing 707s and Douglas DC-8s. And he was bent on making his ideas fly without borrowing money - or taking orders - from the Wall Street financiers.

Entire books have examined his mental decay during this period: how he wore the same white shirt and brown slacks for weeks at a time and spent hours cleaning his telephone. During one stretch Hughes restricted his diet to chocolate bars, nuts, milk and bottled water. He insisted these items be delivered to him daily in a brown paper bag.

By Rummel's account, the Texan resisted the advice of corporate planners and financial experts to the point that Rummel was practically his only confidant at TWA.

Hughes spent 10 hours some nights in meandering phone conversations with Rummel, who had to install a special phone at his Prairie Village home so as not to disturb his sleeping family.

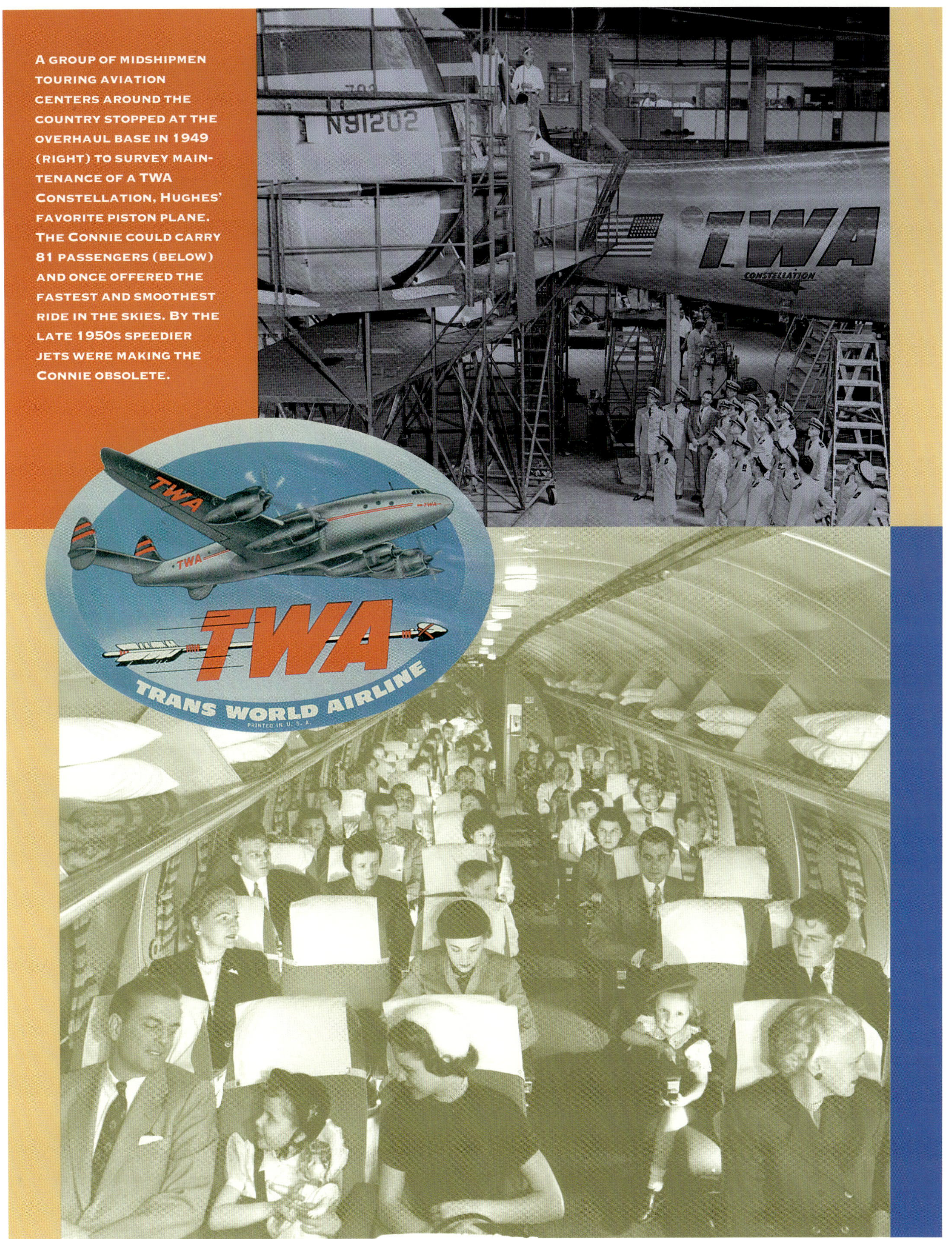

A GROUP OF MIDSHIPMEN TOURING AVIATION CENTERS AROUND THE COUNTRY STOPPED AT THE OVERHAUL BASE IN 1949 (RIGHT) TO SURVEY MAINTENANCE OF A TWA CONSTELLATION, HUGHES' FAVORITE PISTON PLANE. THE CONNIE COULD CARRY 81 PASSENGERS (BELOW) AND ONCE OFFERED THE FASTEST AND SMOOTHEST RIDE IN THE SKIES. BY THE LATE 1950s SPEEDIER JETS WERE MAKING THE CONNIE OBSOLETE.

A TWA public relations man named Gordon Molesworth fell prey to Hughes' weird whims during his first week on the job in Kansas City. Hughes phoned the rookie with orders to fly to Hollywood that day, according to the Hughes biography "Empire" by Donald Barlett and James Steele. Molesworth was to report to Ciro's, a celebrity nightclub, where the head waiter would give him "further instructions."

Molesworth flew there only to be handed ice water and magazines. Hours later, he was told that Hughes no longer needed him. The next day Molesworth flew back to Kansas City, totally confused.

TWA executives came, complained, and went. Even the spirited Damon grew bitter and strained by Hughes' inaction. He died of a heart attack at 58.

When Damon's replacement, Carter Burgess, was named president by Hughes in 1957, a *Star* editorial writer asked at his reception: "So what's Howard Hughes like?"

"I don't know," Burgess confided. "I've never spoken with him."

Burgess quit 11 months later.

By this time Hughes had faced up to the fact that TWA needed jets, period. He ordered 30 from aircraft maker Convair after dropping his demands that they look like "shimmering gold" and be called "golden arrows."

Convair was finishing those jets, Model 880s, in 1959. But

THE 'IDEAL WOMAN'

Clipped Wings group in KC recalls early service with a smile

Walt Disney studios came to Kansas City in 1955 to portray TWA hostesses as radiant role models for a TV series, "When I Grow Up."

Within a few years little girls such as Kathy Moore, whose mother worked for TWA, would corral friends into a narrow hallway to play "airplane stewardess," catering to requests for soda and gum. Other local children dressed up as stewardesses on Halloween.

"We had such pride. But society's different now," Willadean Berglund said a half-century after her four-year ride as a TWA hostess. "I get on a plane now and I feel too critical. Why, after the attendants serve a meal they sit down!"

Forgive her for being critical. It's just that when Berglund and other retired flight attendants gather for luncheons, they talk of when flying was flying - not like riding a bus. Then they'll apologize to you, their guest, and make sure your coffee cup is full.

They are the TWA Clipped Wings, Kansas City chapter. In the spring of 1994 about two dozen members from their 30s to their 70s dined around a U-shaped table at a Mexican restaurant for their monthly session.

Among them: The high-stepper who left the Radio City Rockettes for the pizazz of serving prime rib at 8,000 feet. The hostess who dated pop singer Tony Orlando. The daughter-in-law of Don Ameche, the late actor.

There was Eugenia Cutolo, who waited on TWA passengers when everyone wore a suit or fine dress on board. They handed their coats to her to be tagged and draped on a hanger. Furs were folded inside-out and set on a rack.

And there was Cutolo's daughter, Toni Dodd, who became a flight attendant in a very different era.

She walked past striking TWA picketers in the 1980s to land a hectic job that lacked the glamour so vivid in glossy photographs of her mother at work, she said. Passengers wore shorts, T-shirts, even hair curlers, and many seemed perturbed when asked if they'd like

to read a magazine.

Dodd soon gave it up to study teaching.

Some of the Clipped Wings worked as attendants just a couple of years, even less. That they still were meeting each month spoke to the spirit that binds them: a spirit of service, the best service, with a smile and the expressed hope that you fly TWA again.

"At a time when the country wasn't used to flying," said Berglund, "it was important that we be the P.R. people for the airline."

A decent argument could be made that the good ol' days were flagrantly sexist. For decades, only single young women - recruited from colleges and county fairs nationwide - were invited to the hostess-training school Downtown.

Company rules prohibited them from chewing gum or smoking whenever in uniform, on board a plane or not. They were subjected to "the girdle snap;" a female inspector would suddenly pinch their hips to check for the required girdle. And if they weren't wearing the regulation lipstick, Million-Dollar Red, they flirted with a reprimand.

Hostesses of a half-century ago "were projected as the ideal woman, combining prettiness, good grooming, intelligence, efficiency and self confidence," according to the TWA history book *Wings of Pride*. Brunettes outnumbered blondes 3-to-1. Only 2 percent were redheads.

If any hostess of that era objected to the "ideal woman" stamp, few expressed it. Indeed, their dedication to service in-

cluded one hostess' rush to a post office to mail a transferring passenger's life insurance premium before a midnight deadline.

But the job was redefined by changes in aircraft, not to mention changes in attitude, said former hostess Marie Trainer, who helped compile an archive of the manuals, menus and memorabilia of generations of TWA attendants.

Consider that in 1947, TWA ferried no more than 28 passengers on the Douglas DC-3, about 50 on the Lockheed Constellation. That allowed hostess Wanda Moore of Kansas City, North, to treat all passengers "as if they were guests in my home." Her flight list identified each by name.

Continued on Page 38

Continued from Page 37

She answered their questions about transferring flights or catching a limousine at the airport. She even played cards with a few.

"Isn't it wonderful?" a supervising hostess told Moore as they gazed upon a DC-3 cabin during one of her first flights. "Every one of those passengers has a story to tell you."

But by the time Moore's daughter was a TWA flight attendant (along with several men) in the mid-1970s, the airline could pack 400 people into a Boeing 747. Cruising speeds had doubled, requiring attendants to serve 10 times as many passengers in half the flying time.

If that wasn't grueling enough, by the 1980s - when TWA's Breech Training Academy in Overland Park groomed flight attendants in what the airline called "Travel College" - the curriculum included eight hours of videotaped instructions in how to react to terrorists.

"I think 95 percent of the flight attendants today are still genuinely concerned about their passengers," said Moore's daughter Katherine Grant, the one who played airplane stewardess as a girl. "They just don't have as much time to show it."

And the impressions they leave on youngsters will not likely be as lasting.

The memories were expressed by visitors to a 1996 traveling exhibit of TWA history, which accompanied a Smithsonian Institution display touring the nation.

The old uniforms, the serving plates, the pillbox caps of the 1960s - "I remember!" gasped baby boomers filing through the exhibit. As she eavesdropped, archivist Trainer could only assume that the images were burned into the minds of young passengers who stared for hours and hours at the hostess in the aisle.

A TWA BOOKLET GIVEN TO PASSENGERS IN THE 1960S FEATURED CUT-OUTS OF FLIGHT ATTENDANTS THAT COULD STAND UPRIGHT ON A TABLETOP.

IN THE 1970S MEN JOINED THE RANKS OF TWA FLIGHT ATTENDANTS (PICTURED ABOVE) IN A NEW LINE OF UNIFORMS. A TWA PROMOTIONAL BROCHURE (SHOWN BELOW) TOUTS THE ROLE OF HOSTESSES AND PROMISES "LUXURY LIVING ALOFT."

even Hughes couldn't pay the bill. So he sent armed guards to invade the plant and stop the work. Convair, afraid to offend its biggest customer in Hughes, let him get away with it.

Hughes would let weeks go by before returning phone calls from the TWA brass, even when multimillion-dollar decisions hung in the balance. Unbeknownst to the corporate officers, he had developed a dependence on codeine and other drugs.

Historians would later speculate that Hughes' addictions stemmed from heavy medication prescribed to him in 1946, when he crashed one of his self-designed speed planes.

Morale at TWA hit bottom as the 1950s closed, when Hughes' tool company secured its own jets on borrowed money. The tycoon admonished that "TWA has no rights whatsoever" to them without a lease arrangement, according to a Hughes memo.

When TWA finally launched domestic jet service on Hughes' terms, it had lost $4.5 million in three years on piston planes. Hughes, whose tool company also struggled, had surrendered to the force he hated most - Wall Street lenders - to secure the loans that gave the airline its first jets.

He was forced to put his majority TWA stock in a voting trust as part of a $165 million loan agreement with Equitable Life Assurance, the Irving Bank and Trust Co. and other financiers.

And as the airman's airline burned, Wall Street came through with fire hoses. The men in charge of the Hughes voting trust picked lawyers and corporate wizards to run the airline.

Under terms of the deal, the operation of TWA officially left Hughes' grasp on the final day of 1960.

Wayward flight

In 1961, the airline made its independence from Hughes clear when it filed a $115 million antitrust suit against him and his tool company. The airline alleged that Hughes had tried to set up a monopoly in the sale of jets. Hughes fired back with a lawsuit of his own.

Those lawsuits became among the greatest legal battles of all time, dragging on until 1988. The Delaware Supreme Court ultimately upheld nearly $50 million in damages and interest awarded TWA.

As for Hughes himself, the swashbuckling image eroded to something bizarre. He dropped from public sight in 1957, a drug addict increasingly obsessed with germs.

The man who had romanced Hollywood starlets would see practically nobody but a squadron of male attendants. The man who had ruled an empire would become ruled by madness.

No newsman had seen or heard from the billionaire recluse in 15 years when a mysterious phone call was routed to Kenneth R. Canfield of *The Kansas City Times*' copy desk Jan. 9, 1972, at 8:30 p.m.

The caller demanded to speak with former Editor Roy Roberts. "Tell him it's Howard - Howard from Texas. He'll remember," the caller barked. "Some of us used to get together for a few drinks when I was in town."

Canfield informed him that Roberts had died several years earlier. Then the newsman asked, 'Howard who?" The caller erupted: "Howard who! Don't you really know who this is, boy?"

He identified himself as Howard Hughes, late of TWA, and he wanted to blow the lid on a just-released book purported to be his "autobiography." Canfield later typed up some notes on the conversation: "The voice I heard was old, reedy and with a whiskeyed huskiness." It all conveyed "the self-assuredness of a man not used to having his demands questioned."

The *Times* was suspicious and passed on the story. But soon newspapers around the globe trumpeted news of a similar call made the following day to reporters with *The New York Times* and Associated Press. The dubious "autobiography" of Hughes was on everyone's lips within a week. The book later was found to be a hoax engineered by author Clifford Irving.

Canfield never heard from the mystery caller again, nor did hardly anyone else. "Was it really Howard Hughes..." he pondered in his notes, "or was it only a lonely old man somewhere with no claim to celebrity? I have no idea."

And so it always was with the enigmatic mogul who once called TWA his very own. Hughes died at age 70, a wasted, 90-pound wretch ravaged by time and kidney failure. ✴

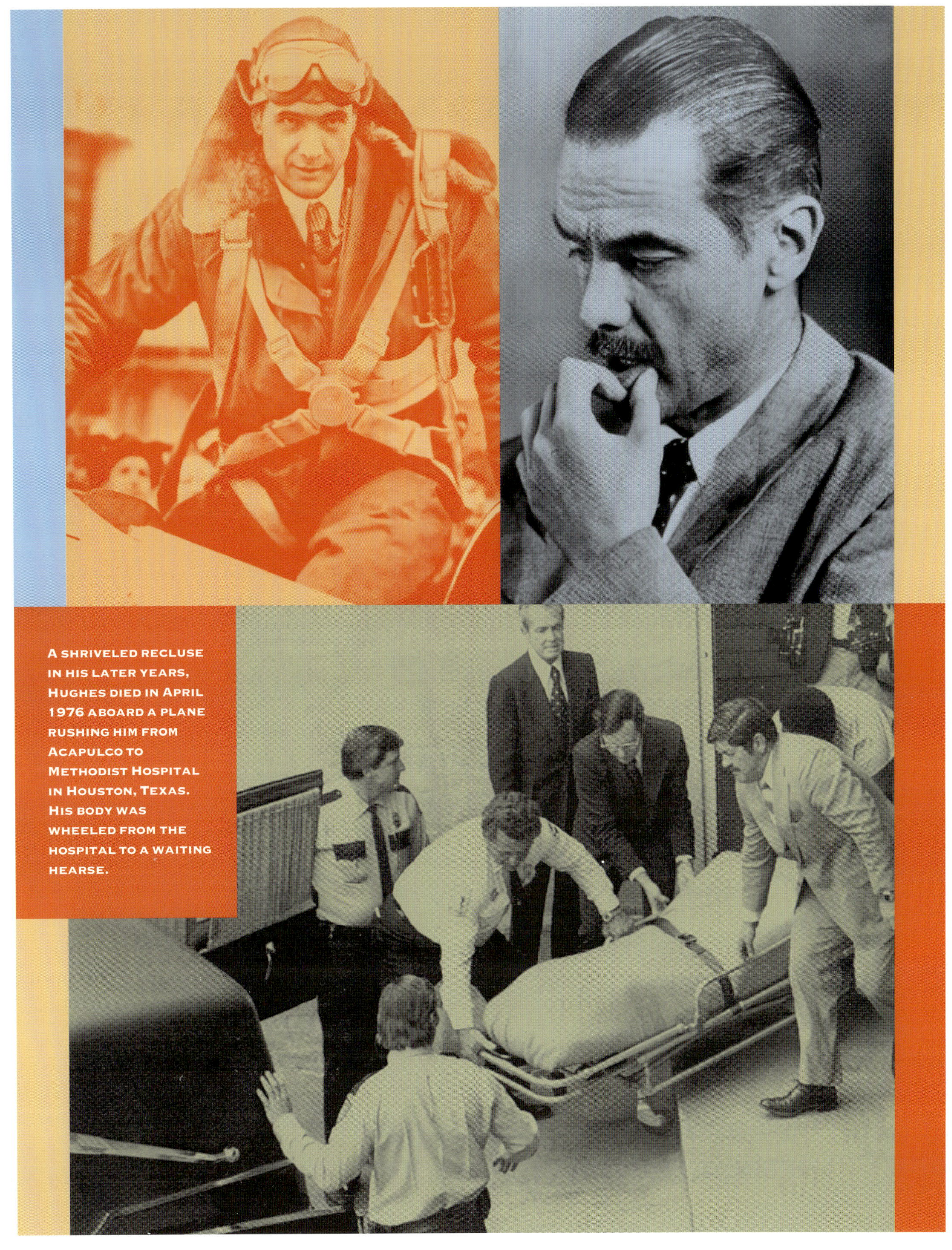

A shriveled recluse in his later years, Hughes died in April 1976 aboard a plane rushing him from Acapulco to Methodist Hospital in Houston, Texas. His body was wheeled from the hospital to a waiting hearse.

CHAPTER 3

THE GLORY YEARS

Downtown basked in the morning sun on April 26, 1962. Along Baltimore Avenue, flags from the 15 nations served by Trans World Airlines snapped in the breeze. ✴ *The short man at the lectern was former president Harry Truman. The huge man, Mayor H. Roe Bartle. Both political heavies stepped back to watch a 9-year-old girl fire a "cloud gun," its white puff christening TWA's flight training center.* ✴ *The airline's new president, Charles C. Tillinghast Jr., flew in from New York to praise the facility. He called it "as close to perfection as modern technology and human ingenuity can make it."* ✴ *This was the jet age. Anything seemed possible.* ✴ *And TWA was setting a 10-year course for glorious, if mythic, horizons.*

Although the airline was late with jets and always vulnerable to industry swings, it had grown in 30 swift years to become Kansas City's largest and most glamorous employer. Its workers enjoyed some of the highest wages in town, plus free travel "up, up and away," as the TWA commercials chimed.

The company dedicated the Baltimore Avenue building to the little girl's daddy, ex-TWA president Jack Frye, who died in a car wreck three years earlier. Frye had broken flight records and helped build futuristic planes despite the airline's struggle to produce profits.

The new boss was Frye's opposite - a corporate lawyer who knew nothing about planes but plenty about the engines of big business. TWA under Tillinghast's command would snap out of fickle cycles of success to post its best years ever. By the 1970s, the airline would pump more than $200 million yearly into the Kansas City economy.

The city would aim high at the same time, unveiling glamorous projects ranging from the Truman Sports Complex to Crown Center to a sprawling international airport next to TWA's Northland overhaul base.

"When TWA people were making lots of money, the enthusiasm in the community absolutely blossomed," said Max Norman, a former Chamber of Commerce executive. "You look at the history of this community. It looks awfully like the history of TWA."

TWA HOSTESSES GATHERED IN 1968 AT AN OVERLAND PARK MOTEL TO SIMULATE BREAKING GROUND FOR A HOSTESS TRAINING ACADEMY THEN UNDER CONSTRUCTION AT U.S. 50 AND LAMAR AVENUE. A PASSENGER SONG-SHEET (BELOW); CHARLES C. TILLINGHAST, JR. (RIGHT).
Be in Europe — Tomorrow!
Your TWA Song Sheet
Fly the Finest...
FLY TWA
TRANS WORLD AIRLINES
TRANS WORLD AIRLINES

The airline lustfully bought the latest jets, not to mention Hilton hotels, Century 21 Realty and Hardee's restaurants - a move to diversify. Airline employment more than doubled between 1958 and 1968, topping off locally at nearly 10,000.

As executives' salaries grew, union pilots and flight attendants took turns demanding fatter cuts of the pie. Overhaul-base workers, pursuing a new contract, even staged a December 1969 slowdown in which they popped makeshift firecrackers and used tools to pound out a rendition of "Jingle Bells."

Between contract talks, executives thought the airline prosperous enough to include a swimming pool and tennis courts in its 34-acre hostess school in Overland Park.

But this party wouldn't last.

Nobody at the 1962 dedication had known then to trumpet the end of TWA's history as "the Airman's Airline," its motto when pilots Frye and Howard Hughes ran the company. The fact was, the airline now belonged to Wall Street lenders.

Decades later, many observers - including ex-TWA bosses - would say the gust of new money transformed a lean, mean company of aviators to a bloated conglomerate of opportunists.

That made TWA ill-prepared for tough times. A cash crunch caused by soaring fuel costs in the mid-1970s forced the carrier to sell jumbo jets to Iran. And by the late '70s,

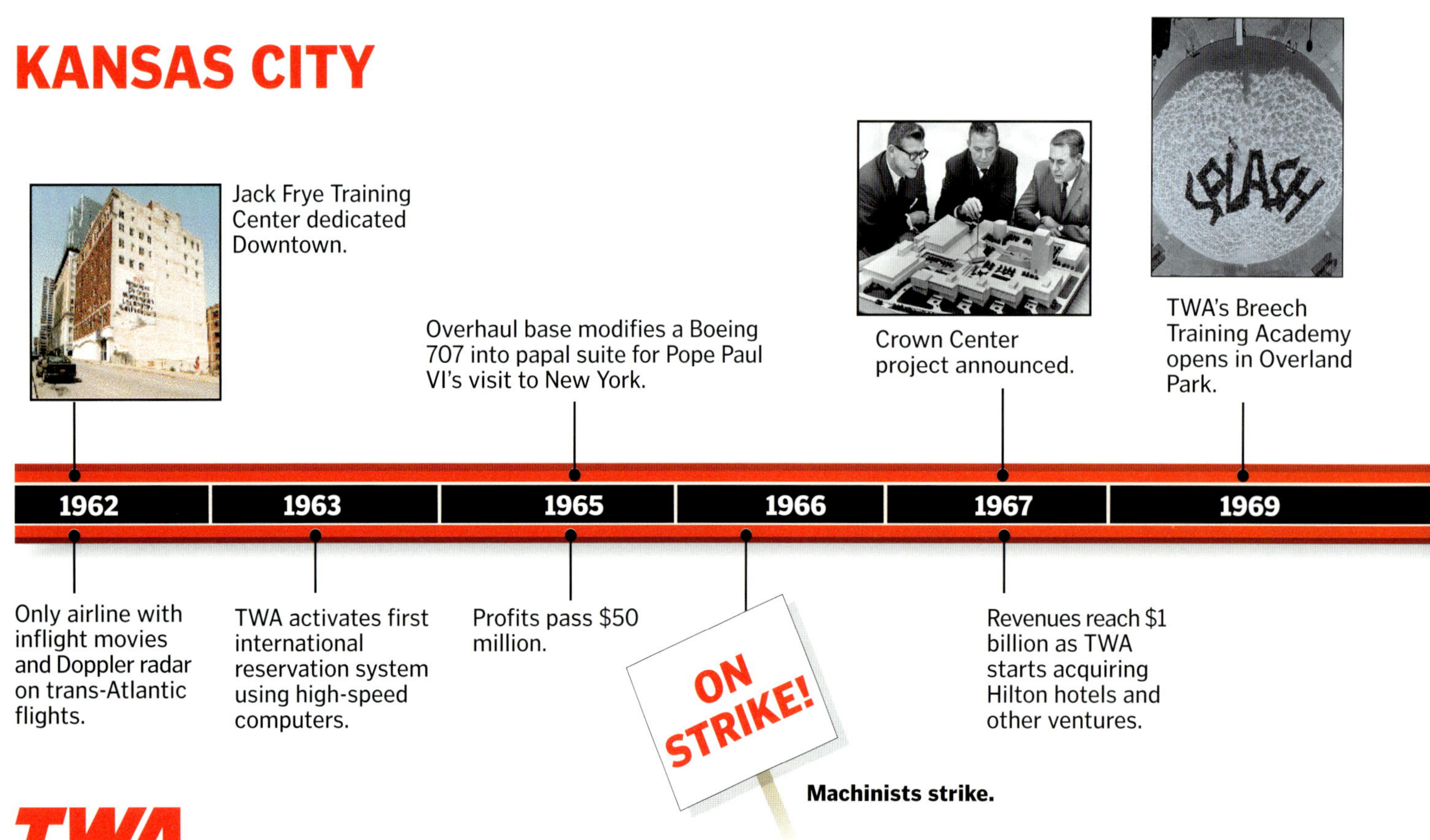

when the federal government deregulated airlines, TWA had lost focus, its portfolio packed with unrelated holdings.

"It just got to be a big-money business," said former Kansas City Mayor Ilus Davis in 1994, two years before his death.

Shift to the east

The transformation began in 1960, when legal action and loans from New York financiers forced the maverick Howard Hughes out of the airline he loved. Entities unknown to Kansas City, such as the Irving Bank and Trust Co., were suddenly mapping TWA's destiny.

A group of these lenders had arranged for a $165 million loan that helped TWA land badly needed jets. But the lenders compelled Hughes to place his majority stock in a voting trust, out of his control.

The lenders picked Ernest Breech to head the trusteeship managing Hughes' shares. Breech had headed the Bendix Corp., maker of missiles, truck brakes and aerospace parts.

He tapped Bendix attorney Tillinghast to be TWA president, and soon, Tillinghast was negotiating a mega-merger with Pan American Airways. "We'll Fulfill Our Destiny - THE Trans World Airline!" proclaimed a headline in TWA's corporate newspaper, but the proposed merger couldn't win government approval.

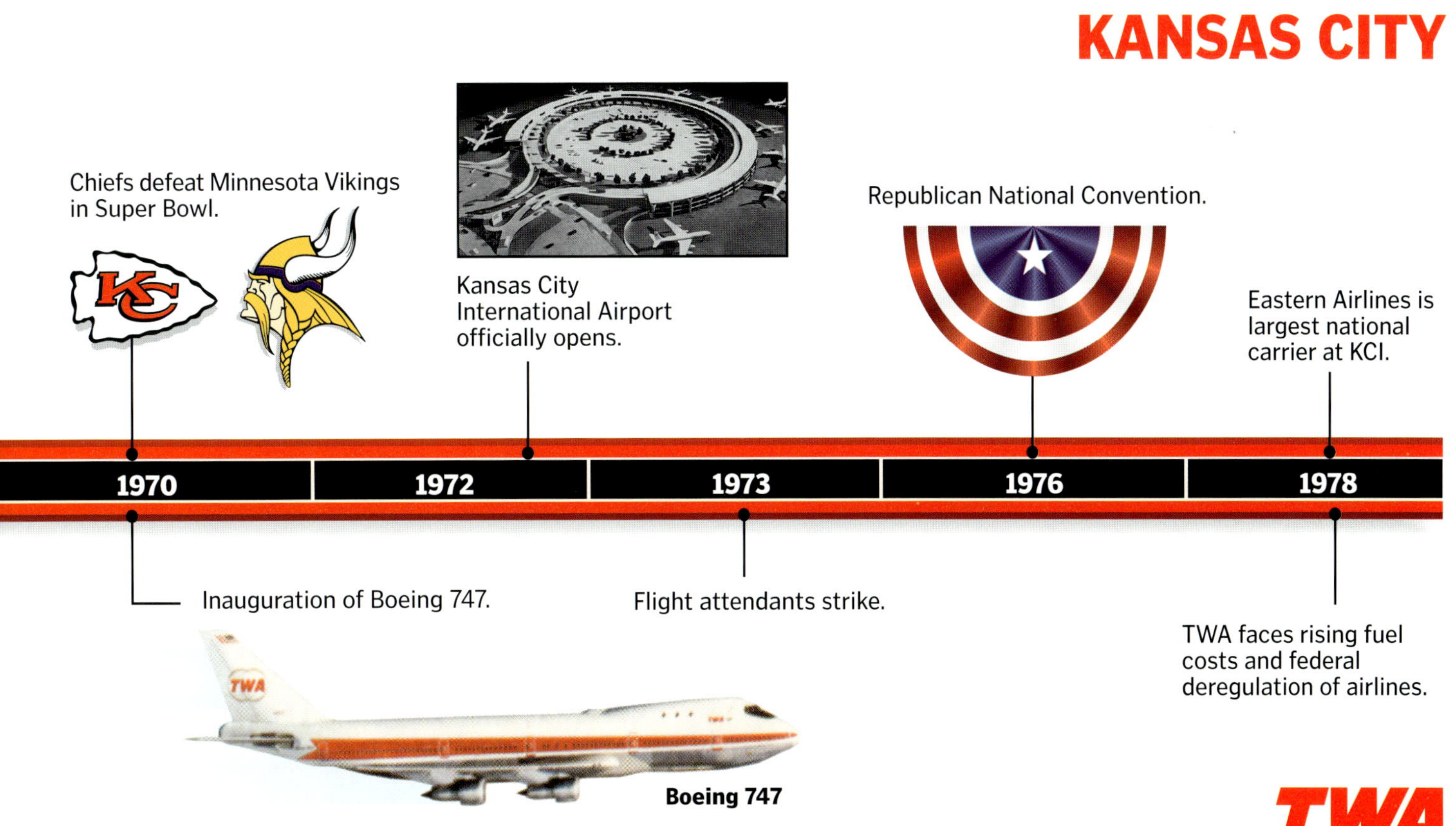

Boeing 747

Tillinghast later relied on another Bendix lawyer, L. Edwin Smart, to mastermind TWA's venture into other industries.

All along the way, the corporation's power center - and its jobs - gradually shifted to the east.

New York was a logical base for a global business such as TWA's. In fact, Kansas City had lost bragging rights to its "hometown airline" years before the new corporate team took over. During World War II TWA set up executive offices in Washington. Its New York division handled much of the international business thereafter.

But it wasn't until the 1960s that Kansas Citians noticed a deliberate, seismic transfer of the airline's management, marketing and reservation offices.

Some 300 jobs were lost in the first half of 1963 - 50 going to a reservations department in St. Louis. Another 100 moved to New York the next year when TWA opened a plush office building there.

The Kansas City Council passed a resolution urging TWA to slow the exodus.

"I never would go," recalled TWA budget manager Charles Smirl of Kansas City, more than 30 years later. "They locked me in a room for two hours trying to convince me that New York was just as affordable as Kansas City."

Former chamber executive Norman said many employees shared Smirl's objections to leaving. "We tried and tried to stop that situation, but it couldn't be stopped," Norman said.

Why not?

"The old excuse," said Richard D. Pearson, an ex-TWA president who started as a data processor in 1967. "Because you needed a lot of capital in an airline, you needed to be where the financial markets were, and obviously that's New York."

The new corporate face of TWA bore little resemblance to that of Hughes. Whereas Hughes had set speed records in his own aircraft, Tillinghast's most memorable flight was a nightmare of delays as a TWA passenger in the 1950s.

As staid and droopy-eyed as Hughes was rumpled and wild-eyed, Tillinghast had flown the airline maybe a half dozen times before agreeing to be its president.

But the Tillinghast reign proved he could turn Hughes' erratic airline into a steady moneymaker. It enjoyed an unbroken string of profits between 1963 and 1969.

"He was the last good president TWA ever had," said airline analyst Morten Beyer.

A romance with jets

The glory years were defined as much by pride as by profits.

"We were the envied ones around town," recalled Warren Berg, who joined the headquarters at 10 Richards Road as a navigational instructor after World War II. He worked up to be director of ground training, landing enough bonuses in the 1960s to send both daughters to college.

"People in our business had a spirit that made me want to get up and go to work," he said. "It was like inventing a new machine. I wanted to get to that machine and make it better that day."

Walt Gunn's 39 years as a TWA pilot put him in every kind of passenger plane from DC-3s to jumbo jets. His fondest memories date to the dawn of the jet age. "Sheer, unadulterated romance," said the native Kansas Citian. "There wasn't a better job

(ABOVE) JETS BECOME COMMON AT TWA. LOCAL MEMBERS OF THE AIR LINE PILOTS ASSOCIATION (RIGHT) UNVEILED A SIGN DOWNTOWN IN 1971 AS PART OF THE UNION'S EFFORTS TO BOOST REVENUES FOR TWA. THE AIRLINE EMPLOYED ABOUT 35,000 PEOPLE WORLDWIDE THAT YEAR.

CHARLES C. TILLINGHAST, JR.

"I finally concluded that airlines were a lousy business."

■ **BORN:** Jan. 30, 1911, in Saxton's River, Vermont.

■ **EDUCATION:** He obtained a Bachelor's degree in philosophy at Brown University in 1932 and a law degree from Columbia University in 1935. More than a half-dozen colleges later awarded him honorary degrees.

■ **PRIOR TO TWA:** He worked in a private law practice before becoming an assistant to New York District Attorney Thomas E. Dewey, who later lost to Harry Truman in the 1948 presidential race. From 1957 to 1961, Tillinghast served as vice president for international operations at the Bendix Corp.

■ **AT TWA:** Selected in 1961 by directors to lead TWA after tycoon Howard Hughes abdicated control, Tillinghast presided over seven straight years of profit and saw the airline's worldwide payroll triple. During a 15-year tenure as president, chief executive officer and, in 1973, chairman, TWA introduced the wide-bodied Boeing 747 but also faced financial crises caused by strikes and soaring fuel costs.

■ **DEPARTURE:** He retired from the airline in 1976, when TWA posted a $30 million profit. He joined an investment banking firm and continued to serve as chancellor and trustee of Brown University, where student activists had tagged Tillinghast "that Wall Street imperialist," despite his many charitable gifts to the college. He died in 1998 at his summer home in Rhode Island.

anywhere ....

"In 1962 TWA had a program called 'This is Your Captain Speaking.' I went to church groups, classrooms and Rotary Clubs telling people about the new jets.

"Oh, they ate up the jets."

So did TWA. Any big jet proved for a time to be a 540-mph cash register. The company's annual revenues reached $1 billion with jets; its worldwide payroll tripled.

The higher fares that accompanied jets spurred TWA to buff up even more the luster of first-class travel. "Royal Ambassador" service offered veal parmesan or beef carved in front of the passengers and served on fine china imported from Germany.

The airline's employees also struck a romance with jet-propelled travel. Families of TWA workers were entitled to free flights anywhere in the system.

Gunn's son flew from Kansas City to Madrid for a haircut.

TWA supervisor Gordon Parkinson once crammed more than 10,000 miles into a four-day weekend. He toured Paris, Ireland and New York just to prove he could.

"That access to the rest of the world gave Kansas City a cultural awareness that most cities our size didn't have," said former chamber executive Norman.

But such perks fostered resentment in some circles toward privileged "airline people," as corporate raider Carl Icahn later labeled them. Even some TWAers whispered "elitism" when they saw rookie co-pilots toting the luggage of certain captains.

Tillinghast said in an interview not long before his death in 1998 that one of his toughest tasks was to balance fiscal needs with the high-mindedness of TWA "prima donnas" and "flyboys," whose view of the

(ABOVE) JETS IN A LINE AT KANSAS CITY INTER-NATIONAL. (LEFT) AT ITS 34-ACRE HOSTESS SCHOOL IN OVERLAND PARK, TWA PUT IN A SWIMMING POOL, TENNIS COURTS AND FACILITIES TO ACCOMMODATE AS MANY AS 4,000 STUDENTS. THIS BOLD WORD WAS PAINTED ON THE BOTTOM OF THE POOL. (BELOW) A TWA REFRESHMENT ON DISPLAY AT THE AIRLINE HISTORY MUSEUM.

airline too often was limited to the cockpit.

"Unless you can find ways to make money, no airline can continue," Tillinghast said.

Former City Council member Bob Lewellen, who spent much of his council career on aviation matters, contends that the corporation itself could be pushy and short-sighted. The city did its best to please, buying nearly 5,000 acres in Platte County for TWA's new overhaul base after the 1951 flood hammered its Fairfax facilities.

Then, in 1966, local voters approved $150 million in revenue bonds to convert the Northland airport - called Mid-Continent International at the time - into the city's main passenger airport, Kansas City International. It opened with runways long enough to handle jumbo jets. Yet TWA decided to locate an air traffic hub in St. Louis instead of Kansas City.

Lewellen acknowledged that Kansas City's airport was not originally designed to be a hub, with lots of connecting flights, but it could have been modified. He charged that TWA "had a direct part in hoodwinking the city leaders into not marketing the airport" to other airlines that were looking for hubs in the 1970s.

Most airlines had established hubs elsewhere by the time Lewellen joined the council in 1983. But even then, he said the city's continued loyalty to TWA hampered his efforts to attract other carriers.

Despite TWA's swagger, profits were not automatic even in the glory years. After earning more than $50 million in 1965, the airline posted losses in the first half of 1968, in 1970 and 1971. The entire industry became more susceptible to strikes, fuel prices, equipment needs, disasters and hijackings.

At a time when federal rules restricted how

PRIDE OF MAINTENANCE

Overhaul base remains vital to Kansas City's economy

The day was just too hot for a formal groundbreaking. Besides, dignitaries would have to drive across dirt to get to the site way up there in Platte County, where no shade or plumbing existed to comfort a crowd.

So at 7 a.m. on July 17, 1954, a stout crew from the Clarkson Construction Co. decided on its own to get cracking on what proved to be a truly historic project for Trans World Airlines, and for Kansas City. An article inside *The Kansas City Star* that afternoon reported:

"Without ceremony, on a corner of a 4,590-acre site in Platte County, 20 men began turning dirt today."

The result was not only the TWA overhaul base, where three generations of workers would punch in and take home more than $100 million in annual salaries by century's end. Just as important, those first bucketfuls of dirt also marked the beginning of an airfield that evolved into Kansas City International Airport.

At its maintenance shop 18 miles north of Downtown, the airline enjoyed two things its old facilities couldn't provide: a long runway and high, dry ground.

The city purchased the undeveloped land in the early 1950s for an average $354 per acre, then issued $18.7 million in revenue bonds for construction. TWA signed a 30-year lease to occupy the building. Considered the state of the art, it sported a cantilevered roof that grabbed the notice of architectural journals around the world.

It was the overhaul workers' third and most enduring home. In 1946 they moved out of hangars at Municipal Airport, then located just north of downtown, to occupy part of the North American Aviation plant in the Fairfax District of Kansas City, Kan. The flood of 1951 swallowed those facilities, where bombers had been built during World War II.

Perhaps it's fitting that the groundbreaking for the Northland base drew no dignitaries. The thousands of Kansas

Citians who have kept TWA's fleet humming - mechanics, engineers, hydraulic specialists, electricians, sheet-metal workers, painters and radio technicians - always toiled behind the scenes of "the airline of the stars."

But the overhaul workers' industry-topping performance clearly kept TWA in business through the decades.

When the 1990s arrived, TWA was making do with the most aged fleet in the industry. Two-thirds of its jets were more than 15 years old. All were pulled into the Kansas City shop every few years for the all-encompassing "D" check, in which an entire aircraft is stripped, inspected, modified, cleaned and repaired in six weeks.

The base not only withstood the rigors of servicing TWA's older aircraft. It also produced revenue by performing contract work on planes owned by other carriers.

Following decades of labor disputes and layoffs, the facility's workforce in 2001 numbered about 2,500 - similar to when it opened in the 1950s.

As aircraft grew wider and longer, the base stretched far enough to cover 43 football fields. But employment would dwindle after approaching 9,000 in the early 1970s.

Layoffs hit more than 800 base workers in 1992 alone. A mechanic who was bumped back to janitor at the time recalled for *The Star* how TWA took care of its own when his father worked at the base, "but it hasn't quite panned out that way for me and my family."

His 5-year-old daughter that year asked, "Daddy, what's a layoff?"

For each job lost at the base, economic development experts in Platte County estimated that four other jobs disappeared from surrounding restaurants, stores and dry cleaners. All had come to rely on the high paychecks of the maintenance base.

Industry analysts in 2001, reacting to a potential buyout of TWA, expected those paychecks to remain in the Northland, maybe even multiply. Voters the year before had approved the issuance of $110 million in revenue bonds to renovate the facility - an appealing option for any suitor looking to expand its fleet.

David Levine, contributing editor to the online newsletter PlaneBusiness.com, offered up the rosiest of possibilities.

"In 18 months, Kansas City could be doing double the work it has now," said Levine, a veteran follower of TWA history, in January 2001. Though the future was any pundit's guess, the past sold Levine on "the good reputation that the Kansas City shop has."

much airlines could charge customers, Wall Street's brightest hatched a plan to cushion the boom-and-bust nature of airlines.

They called it "diversification," based on the notion that airlines could make themselves immune from crushing losses if they expanded into ventures other than flying.

Other theorists would come up with "deregulation." When applied to airlines, it meant getting government out of the business of controlling routes and fares in hopes of bolstering air travel.

Neither theory would help TWA in the long run.

The distraction of mergers

For a while TWA was the king of airline innovation. In 1961 it introduced in-flight movies. In 1962 it installed the first Doppler radar system on international flights, nixing the need for a navigator on board.

In 1965 a Kansas City maintenance crew converted a Boeing 707 into a suite for Pope Paul VI. It included an altar, a decorative cross donated by an employee and a compartment for traveling media.

In 1970 TWA unveiled the wide-bodied Boeing 747 at a big ceremony in New York.

But then aircraft breakthroughs seemed to cease across the land. Corporate chiefs instead absorbed themselves in diversification. For its part, TWA merged with the Hilton International chain in 1967. In 1973 TWA acquired Canteen Corp., the vending machine firm. And under the direction of TWA Chairman Smart, the corporation unloaded $82 million in cash to buy a company that owned Hardee's Restaurant franchises.

"These were people who weren't trying to run an airline, they were trying to run a business," said former TWA vice chairman Glenn R. Zander.

Management "focused on selling hamburgers and Coke" and not on carrying passengers, he said.

TWA wasn't the only airline to diversify. But airline analyst Scott Hamilton said the move hurt TWA more than others. Its executives "were not as astute in the airline business as the senior management at American and United," he said.

C.E. Meyer Jr., a TWA president of the late 1970s, later acknowledged: "In retrospect, I would say the diversification did distract from the main objective of running an airline."

Without that distraction, TWA might have worked out a better strategy to handle one of its fundamental problems, a shortage of domestic routes, Meyer said.

"We tried everything but standing on our head," he said. "We massaged, changed …. "

They tried gimmicks. TWA once pitched a failed campaign to suit up flight attendants in paper togas to reflect the cultures of other nations. By the late 1960s, the hostesses were sporting hot pants under their jackets.

And speed wars, which once defined the competition, gave way to "lounge wars," best illustrated when American Airlines installed a piano bar on 747 flights.

Disputes inside TWA didn't help. Flight attendants in 1973 walked off their jobs over contract problems, and the timing couldn't have been worse. The Arab oil cartel inflated TWA's fuel prices during the strike from 12 cents per gallon to nearly 50 cents.

Other airlines had wrangled long-term fuel contracts in the interim, undercutting TWA's costs. Zander cited that setback as the

(ABOVE) THE BOEING 747 COMES TO TWA JUST YEARS BEFORE FUEL PRICES SURGED (RIGHT). FLIGHT ATTENDANTS ON STRIKE (BELOW).

beginning of the end of the glory years.

Tillinghast, who retired from TWA about that time and served as chancellor of Brown University, was more blunt: "I finally concluded that airlines were a lousy business."

Deregulatory turbulence

It wouldn't be long before the rules changed again for TWA.

U.S. airlines had always operated like regulated utilities. Fares and routes were decreed by government bureaucrats, sometimes over the objections of airline executives. But in 1978, Washington turned the industry upside down by declaring that airlines would now be deregulated.

The news jolted TWA and other big carriers "like a bolt of lightning," said Zander, who by 2001 would be heading Aloha Airlines in Hawaii. "Here everybody was running around trying to compete on whether you had a 2-inch-steak or a 1-inch-thick steak. ... All of a sudden, BOOM!

"This (new competition) comes in and says, 'Hey, we'll take you from Buffalo to New York City for 30 bucks.' Nobody had heard of such a thing before."

A pack of upstart airlines took to the skies. They hired pilots and other employees for less money. They charged cut-rate fares.

Prime rib gave way to peanuts.

"It was scary," said Bob McAdoo, a former TWA executive who co-founded upstart People Express Airlines in 1980. "You were starting from scratch with a relatively modest amount of capital, compared to the deep pockets the well-established carriers had.

"We also saw the opportunities to build a route system that served only those cities we wanted to serve, in the manner we wanted to

WORKERS' LOYALTY

Atmosphere 'like family' despite financial turmoil

Some people retire from a company, grab the nearest 9-iron and never look back.

Not Tom Perry, who used to fix cockpit instruments for TWA. He spends his retirement collecting company relics - pilots' pins, tattered repair manuals, even slippers worn by passengers - that once filled a display case at the overhaul base.

"It was family," Perry says about his ex-comrades. "You very rarely saw people leave TWA on their own."

For Perry and thousands of other area residents, being a TWAer meant more than earning a paycheck and enjoying free flights on vacation.

The aviation business is steeped in *esprit de corps*, but TWAers shared "a state of mind" unique even among airlines, said aviation author Robert Serling.

Consider:

■ Plugging his former employer to 24,488 baseball fans, retired pilot Harold Neumann jumped into his own plane in 1982 and sky-wrote "Fly TWA " over Royals Stadium. After performing aerobatics well into his 80s, Neumann passed away in 1995.

■ Joy Preston was a stewardess all of eight months in 1961 but still attends monthly luncheons of the local Clipped Wings, an organization of retired TWA flight attendants.

■ The late Gordon Parkinson of Kansas City, North - "Mr. TWA" to his comrades - saluted the company color by wearing a red tie to work every day for 35 years. When he retired as operational planning manager in 1968, he spent his Christmas savings on his own farewell billboard: "Thank You for Flying TWA."

■ Ed Betts, a retired pilot in California, boasts a personal archive of pictures, company memos and countless interviews with TWA colleagues that fill a 5-pound book, "The Making of an Airline."

This isn't just loyalty.

"It's a throwback to an older way of doing business," said Pete D. Nugent, associate professor of industrial relations at Rockhurst College.

Years ago when you worked for giants such as TWA, GM or IBM, he said, "It was almost guaranteed employment. ... You were an IBMer."

TWA RETIREE TOM PERRY NOW COLLECTS AIRLINE MEMORABILIA. "IT WAS A FAMILY."

Aviation experts point to TWA's heritage as an "Airman's Airline" to explain much of the in-house loyalty. In the early years, workers admired the men at the helm - true aviators such as Jack Frye and Howard Hughes. "They pioneered so many things," Serling said.

Through seven decades of buffeting balance sheets, furloughs, power struggles, merger talks, bitter strikes and bankruptcy hearings, that family feeling somehow endured - "like tempered steel," said former TWA spokesman Jerry Cosley, who worked for the company off and on from 1960 until the mid-'90s.

Of course, TWA had its share of family feuds. During labor negotiations in 1969, Machinists protested almost daily outside the overhaul base. Their union even sued TWA in an effort to stop a company-wide "happiness campaign," which entitled good workers to cash, color TVs and movie projectors. TWA awarded sports cars that year to three of its happiest employees.

The Machinists union claimed in the suit that its members weren't all that content (especially during contract talks), and that the airline had no business promoting happiness, anyway.

But Richard M. Steers, a professor of management and vice provost of international affairs at the University of Oregon, said good vibes in the workplace can reap benefits. "If you have strong group cohesiveness, people tend to be more creative, they tend to put forth more effort," he said.

Just ask Avery Dickson, who labored 35 years as a TWA mechanic in Kansas City. The Raymore resident said he and his fellow mechanics used to have a motto: "Good better best. Never let it rest. Till your good is better and your better best."

Then in the mid-1980s came the bottom-line leadership of Carl Icahn, a corporate monster in the near-unanimous view of the TWA tribe. They complained he wasn't an "aviation man;" he was just a businessman.

He wanted to discontinue the free flights for TWA employees. His associates talked him out of it, fearing the move would pummel morale.

"If you said the word 'morale' (to Icahn), you want to settle in for a long winter's tirade," said Glenn R. Zander, former TWA vice chairman who worked closely with Icahn. "His view of morale was, 'I give you a check, you do your job.' Boom."

serve them," said McAdoo, who moved on to establish Kansas City-based Vanguard Airlines in 1994.

But what a wallop for the old-time carriers - especially TWA, which built its reputation on pampering movie stars.

Looking back from the year 2001, ex-pilot Gunn argued that deregulation was largely to blame for the decline of TWA:

"The greatest fallacy was it (deregulation) would increase competition by allowing new entry, easier entry" into the industry, he said. "There were 17 major airlines prior to deregulation and now you can count them on one hand. The air transport industry has become an oligopoly."

The big airlines reacted differently in their brave new industry.

American, led by former TWA employee Bob Crandall, acquired new jets and routes and expanded its computer reservations system. It persuaded its unions to adopt a two-level wage system.

TWA cut fares and expanded international service. It increased flights out of St. Louis. The airline responded "as well as we could," said then-president Meyer.

But TWA veteran Pearson said the soft-spoken Meyer, though fair and intelligent, wasn't tough enough to ram through the changes TWA needed. "It frustrated all of us. We couldn't get work rule changes, couldn't get lower starting wages for new employees,"

said the man who managed the Kansas City overhaul base in the late 1970s.

Gary Poos, general chairman of Machinists District 142 in Kansas City, said the unions weren't to blame.

"The unions wanted TWA to put those hundreds of millions of dollars back into new equipment, new airplanes," Poos said. "Management was putting it into Hilton Hotels, Century 21. ... As a union, we felt we were the ones generating that money for TWA and the other airlines, and we wanted our cut."

By the 1980s, the holding company known as Trans World Corp. would cut the airline loose with an aged fleet, weak domestic routes and devalued stock, allowing corporate raider Carl Icahn to gobble up the scraps.

Today, the Baltimore Avenue building where Jack Frye's daughter fired the cloud gun stands empty - a tarnished symbol of the former TWA.

It was bought in the early '90s by followers of the Indian spiritual leader the Maharishi Mahesh Yogi, but their plans to establish a learning center there never materialized.

The building also was included in elaborate plans to create a vibrant Power & Light District, which also never materialized.

Through locked glass doors still displaying the red TWA logo, a passerby in 2001 sees litter in the foyer that has sat virtually undisturbed for years.

The rotting Hotel President next door, where the TWA brass used to toast, has been shut down for decades.

And transients of the 21st century shuffle daily across a cracked parking lot where Truman, Bartle and Tillinghast once spoke of glory. ✶

TODAY, THE BALTIMORE AVENUE BUILDING (ABOVE) STANDS EMPTY, AS DOES THE ROTTING HOTEL PRESIDENT (RIGHT) WHERE TWA BRASS ONCE TOASTED GOOD TIMES.

CHAPTER 4

A ROUGH LANDING

"Is the deal closed? Is it closed?" ✱ *Corporate raider Carl C. Icahn impatiently barked the question to his financial lieutenants.* ✱ *It was nighttime on Jan. 8, 1993. Icahn's fitful reign at the helm of TWA was about to end.* ✱ *Cued by the tap of a few keystrokes, computers soon would electronically pump $150 million from Icahn's cash hoard to TWA's meager coffers.*

The transfer would cement a crucial agreement among Icahn, TWA and the federal agency that guarantees pensions. Icahn would let go of the carrier he had led - some would say dragged - through seven stormy years. The government agency would halt its dogged pursuit of Icahn over TWA's underfunded pensions.

When word of the transfusion got through, Icahn gleefully danced about his opulent office in Mt. Kisco, N.Y.

"The king is dead! The king is dead!" he shouted, his hawklike eyes turning to Glenn R. Zander, then a top TWA executive.

"And you're Robespierre!" Icahn pronounced, referring to the guillotined French revolutionary. "They'll cut your head off about a year from now."

"That's probably right," replied the stoic Zander, who later would resign his vice chairmanship after losing a management power struggle.

But on that fateful day in January, the long-embattled airline was at peace. Against all odds, it had survived yet another brush with death. And, like Icahn, many of the airline's employees felt like dancing.

Unfortunately, the peace wouldn't last much longer than the dance.

Many TWA workers chafed under Icahn's blunt management style. But he was right about one thing: The former "airline of the stars" had to slash costs to survive in the rough-and-tumble, deregulated world of aviation.

The painful lesson was still being learned in the summer of 1995, as TWA embarked on its second trip through bankruptcy court.

Awash in red ink

It was a hot June day in Beirut in 1985. A jittery terrorist, part of a group that hijacked an Athens-to-Rome flight, held a gun to the sweating head of TWA pilot John Testrake.

The picture of the helpless pilot at his cockpit window dominated front pages and TV screens around the globe.

Rarely had one event so terrified people contemplating overseas trips. America's air-

A Princeton philoso-
phy major turned
corporate raider,
Carl C. Icahn emerged
as a predator bent
on TWA in 1985. He
became chairman in
1986 and, two years
later, took the airline
private in a deal that
enriched Icahn and
saddled the carrier
with huge debts. He
enraged union mem-
bers, led TWA into its
first bankruptcy in
1992 and left in 1993.

lines were now symbolic targets of the terrorist front. Travelers avoided U.S. carriers.

Once again, TWA suffered from rotten timing. Testrake's plight not only exacerbated TWA's troubles but was a stark metaphor for the airline. TWA was sloshing in red ink, suffering with one of the highest operating costs of any airline. Its Kansas City employment had withered to 7,000, down from about 10,000 in 1979. More cutbacks loomed ahead.

Trans World Corp. had jettisoned the airline the previous year, turning TWA into vulture bait.

The spinoff "left the airline very naked," said Richard D. Pearson, a TWA veteran who served briefly as the airline's president in the mid-'80s. "Because now it's this entity by itself, with no real financial resources from the holding company. ... That drove the market price down."

Enter Icahn, the Princeton philosophy major turned corporate raider. He and his investment companies began mounting assaults in the mid-1970s to take control of corporations, often on a hostile basis.

"The problem you've got in America is that management, with many exceptions, is lacking in ability," Icahn told a magazine reporter in 1984. "The chairman of a company will appoint someone who has been his buddy for 25 years as the guy to replace him. He all too often doesn't appoint someone who's really able, because he sees that kind of person as a threat. It's a feudal system."

And by forcing out executives of companies that were, at best, marginally profitable, Icahn said he was acting in the best interests of their owners.

Not everyone agreed. In February 1985, about 40 residents of Bartlesville, Okla.,

gathered in a park to burn proxy statements from Icahn, who was making a bid for Bartlesville-based Phillips Petroleum at the time.

In May 1985, in filings with the Securities and Exchange Commission, Icahn revealed that he had bought 20.5 percent of TWA's stock. He said he was considering whether to seek control of the carrier.

The Icahn announcement struck a sour note with C.E. Meyer Jr., TWA's president and chief executive, who called the Icahn investment "uninvited and undesirable."

Meyer said the financier's "objectives and tactics, his purchase of a large number of our shares and his threat under certain circumstances to seek control of the company are disruptive to our business and not in the best interests of TWA shareholders, employees or the traveling public and communities we serve."

Airline analyst Bob McCormick warned that TWA was "not prepared" for an unfriendly takeover battle because the airline had only a "minimal" number of anti-takeover provisions.

McCormick noted that TWA lacked the financial muscle to "completely stifle" Icahn, mainly because the airline had been struggling to generate profits and was burdened with heavy debts.

"Fighting off someone like Icahn will be very difficult," McCormick predicted.

Within days, TWA filed a petition with the U.S. Department of Transportation that questioned Icahn's ability to run an airline. Specifically, TWA contended that Icahn:

■ Had a history of disruptive business practices and legal entanglements.

■ Had a history of non-compliance with statutory and administrative rules and in-

(Right) Some TWA jets were up for sale in the '80s as a financial move. (Below) Richard D. Pearson, former TWA president. The spinoff "left the airline very naked."

volvement in other disciplinary proceedings.

■ Was unfamiliar with the airline business.

■ Did not have an adequate plan for successfully operating the airline.

TWA also filed lawsuits against Icahn's takeover bid in a Missouri state court and in a New York federal court.

Critics said an Icahn takeover would trigger the dismantling of TWA.

"Even a casual student of this guy's background can read that he doesn't bring a lot to the party that reflects anything like the traditions and sacrifice that have built this airline and this industry," former TWA spokesman Jerry Cosley said at the time. "Pure and simple, he's a wrecking ball looking for something to knock down."

Missouri attempted to defend TWA from Icahn, passing legislation designed to bring an out-of-state company under provisions of a strict state law dealing with hostile takeovers.

"We are taking this unprecedented action today to ensure that Missouri's interests are protected when these hostile takeover bids threaten the Missouri economy," then Gov. John Ashcroft said after signing the bill into law.

TWA tried to find a buyer to top Icahn's $600 million offer for the company. Icahn, saying he wanted a "level playing field," lashed out at TWA directors and officials

KANSAS CITY

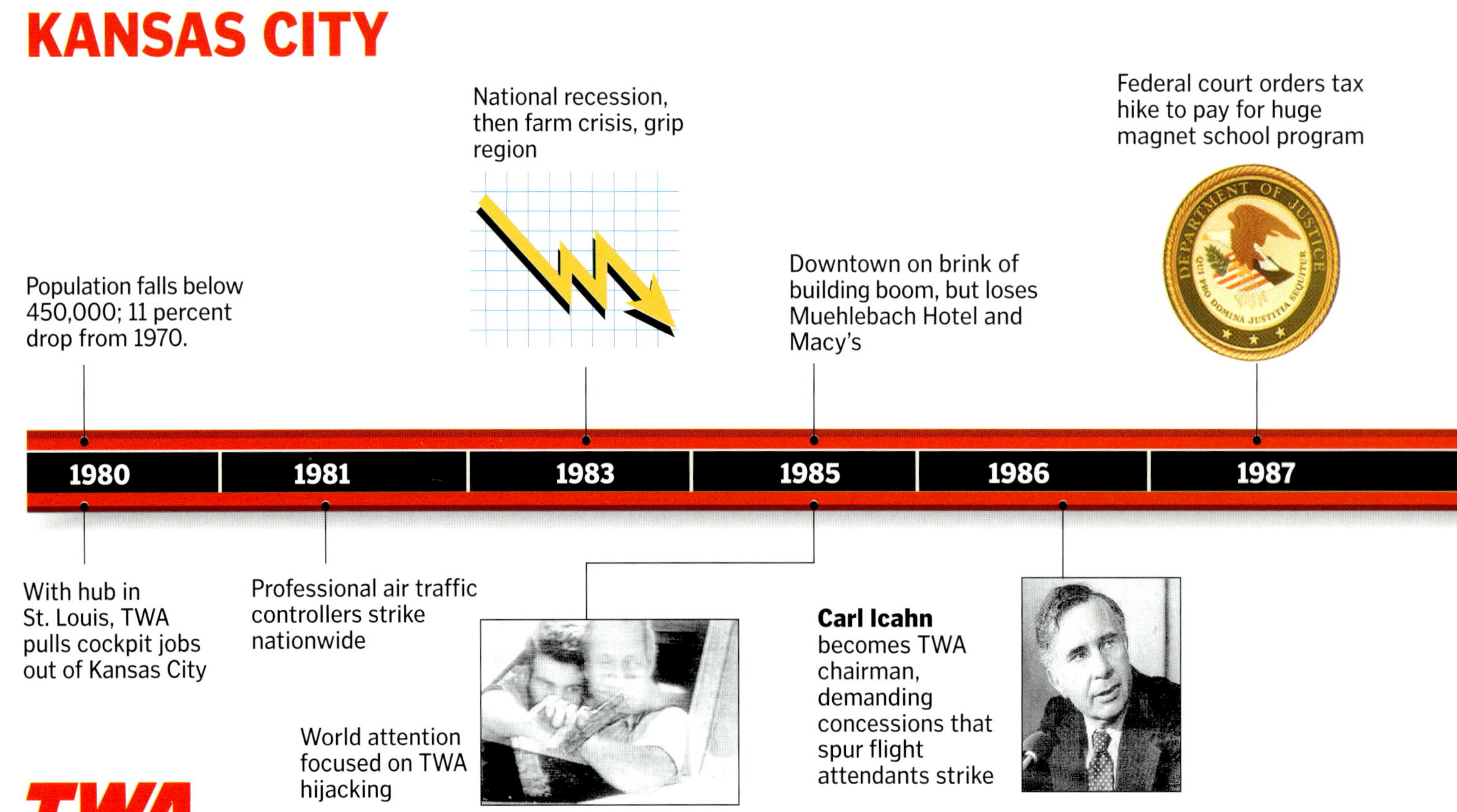

over the airline's plans to handle his and other takeover offers.

A battle for TWA ensued between Icahn and Frank Lorenzo's Texas Air Corp. The corporate raider was supported by unions who feared Lorenzo's notorious anti-labor tactics. Pilots and Machinists agreed to wage concessions.

Icahn won out. As 1986 dawned, he held 52 percent of TWA's common stock and he assumed the chairmanship and control of TWA's board. He had dropped his effort to totally buy out the airline after TWA had drastically raised estimates of its 1985 loss.

But the white knight's suit was a poor fit for Icahn, who eyed bloated budgets the way Carry Nation eyed saloons.

Icahn saw TWA as a "company that had been run in a very lackadaisical, almost country club atmosphere," Zander recalled. "And he took actions, I think, to try to shock people out of that kind of laid-back approach."

Icahn soon found himself at loggerheads with TWA's labor groups.

The unions contended that Icahn was squeezing workers and trying to sell off the airline piecemeal. Flight attendants picketed his house during a 1986 strike and continued to use that tactic during subsequent labor battles.

Icahn insisted he was doing what he had to do to keep TWA off the airline obituary page. He achieved financial successes his

KANSAS CITY

Braniff Airlines, with local hub, files for bankruptcy

High-tech firms such as U.S. Sprint seen as major employers of coming decade

Downtown attracts computer maker Gateway 2000

TWA has about 4,000 workers here, down roughly 60 percent from late '70s.

1989 | **1990** | **1991** | **1992** | **1994** | **1995**

Icahn sells London routes

TWA files for federal bankruptcy protection; Icahn later resigns

TWA optimistically pursues another bankruptcy

TWA London postcard

CARL C. ICAHN

"Although we acted in our own self interest, corporate activists clearly improved the productivity of American business, boosting earnings and stock market valuations, which have enriched millions of American households."

■ **BORN:** 1936, Queens, N.Y.

■ **EDUCATION:** B.A. Princeton University, where he majored in philosophy. Subsequently dropped out of New York University School of Medicine and joined the Army, where he acquired a penchant for gambling. He left the service with $4,000 in poker winnings.

■ **PRIOR TO TWA:** Launched Wall Street career in 1961 with Dreyfus & Co. Borrowed $400,000 to buy a seat on the New York Stock Exchange and started Icahn & Co. Inc. in 1968. Began mounting assaults in the mid-1970s to take control of corporations, often on a hostile basis.

■ **AT TWA:** Icahn unleashed a takeover battle for TWA in 1985 and became chairman of the airline in 1986. Took the airline private in a 1988 deal that sucked $610.3 million out of TWA, of which $469 million went to Icahn. The deal added $539.7 million to the airline's debt.

■ **DEPARTURE:** Led TWA into its first bankruptcy in 1992 and left the company in 1993. Remained a major creditor of the carrier and held a lucrative arrangement to sell discount airline tickets.

first few years, aided by employee concessions and a strong economy. TWA bought Ozark Airlines in 1986 and became the dominant carrier at St. Louis.

The airline earned a record profit of $106.2 million in 1987, after losing an almost identical amount the previous year.

"TWA's dramatic turnaround in 1987 from an airline in trouble to one of the most profitable in the industry is proof that takeovers can and do work," Icahn boasted in his letter to shareholders in TWA's 1987 annual report. "I have been happy to see my theories become realities."

The airline earned record profits again the next year. But much of those earnings were due to TWA's holdings in Texaco Inc. and nearly $50 million it won from a lawsuit filed 27 years earlier against Howard Hughes.

In September 1988, TWA stockholders approved Icahn's proposal to take the airline private.

Strictly for money

The airline soon returned to its money-losing ways. Icahn's complex privatization sucked $610.3 million out of TWA - of which $469 million went to Icahn - and added $539.7 million to the carrier's debt.

Cash interest payments on the higher debt would cut into the bottom line in the early '90s, when TWA and other airlines were reeling from a recession and the Gulf War.

Part of the problem was where Icahn cut costs. When he got chintzy on items such as food and beverage service, frequent trans-Atlantic flyers deserted TWA for other carriers.

Frantically searching for more cuts, Icahn

(Right) Members of Machinists Local 1650 were at odds with Icahn during most of his tenure, constantly battling over labor issues.

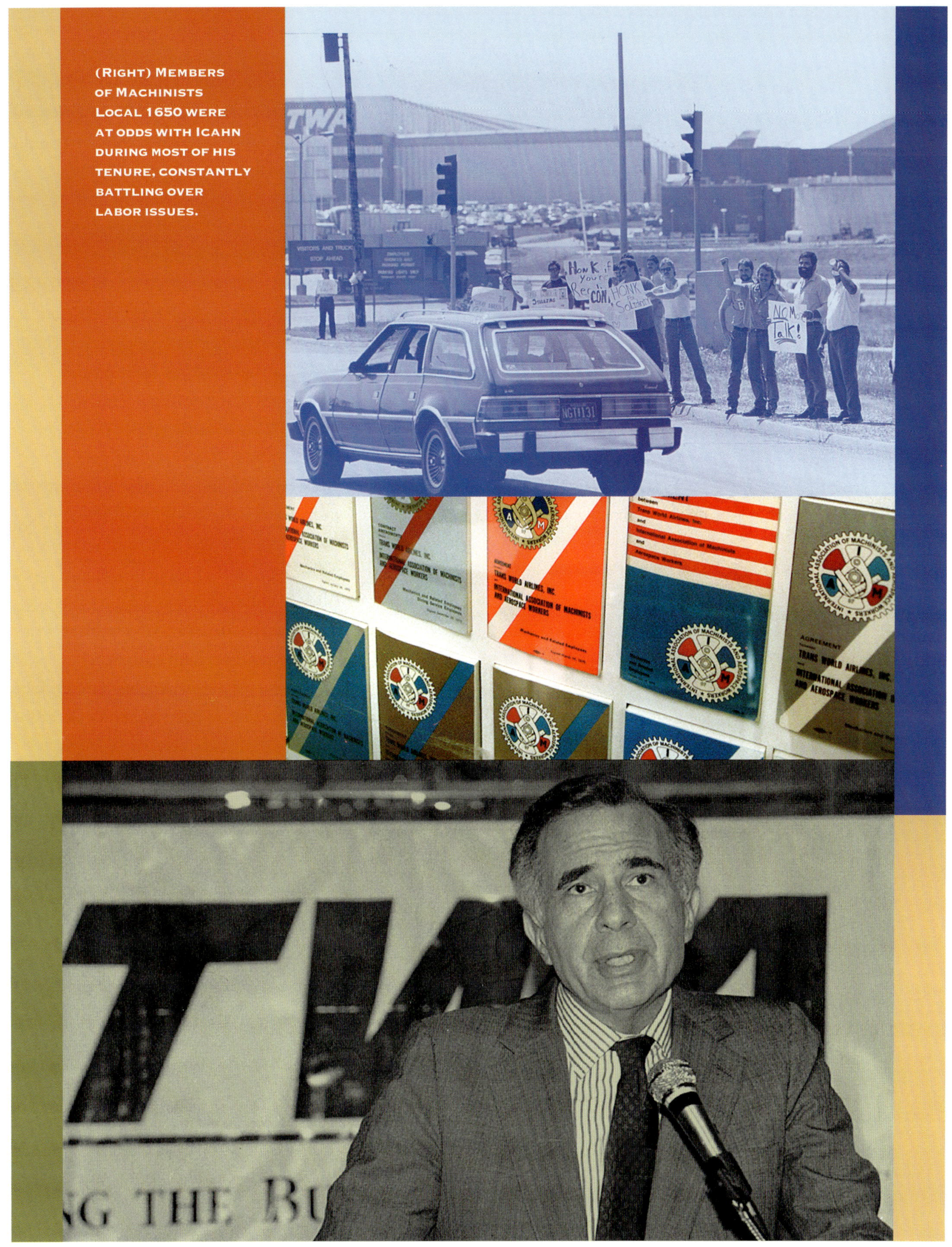

would order studies. What would happen, for instance, if the St. Louis hub were abandoned?

"Carl was immensely frustrated by this business," Zander said. "Carl's mentality is one of logic. He wanted pilots to accept lower salaries because competitors were getting pilots at lower salaries. But the pilots would say no. It drove him crazy."

(Icahn could not be reached for comment for this book after several attempts to interview him.)

TWA had known labor strife before Icahn arrived. But Icahn's new attitude toward labor, exemplified by his crushing of a 1986 flight attendants strike, soon inspired hatred in many of his workers. Employees feared he would sell the airline off piece by piece - such as when he sold prized London routes to American Airlines in 1991.

"I don't think Icahn came to TWA with the idea of harming it," said Herb Johnson, former president of Machinists Local 1650 in Kansas City. "I think he got into it strictly for money and nothing else. That's the real world, that's business."

Looking back, Johnson said he believed the unions were right to help Icahn get control of TWA. After all, the alternative was Lorenzo, notorious for the bad labor relations he fostered at Eastern and Continental.

"We believe Frank Lorenzo was out there to break the trade union movement in the airline industry," Johnson said. "Carl Icahn was strictly a Wall Street money merchant."

Former City Councilman Bob Lewellen, who spent much of his council time on aviation matters, recalled a meeting where Icahn discussed possible route changes. Icahn scoffed at the idea of pilots not wanting to be stuck at an airport all day.

"He was taken aback that it mattered, that anybody would give a damn, that these guys were different than anybody else and would feel bad if they weren't flying all day," Lewellen said. "Kind of like the owner of a sports team who doesn't understand the idiosyncrasies of the players."

Zander, who became TWA's chief financial officer in 1990, frequently opposed Icahn's schemes for the airline. Icahn may not have liked what he heard, but he listened.

"Glenn is very even-tempered," said Richard Shuyler, also a former TWA chief financial officer. "He's just the type of person who is able to handle the type of crisis management that was going on at TWA at that time. ... He didn't let Icahn intimidate him."

Zander, now the president and chief executive of Aloha Airlines in Hawaii, contends TWA "was heading for a fall whether Carl Icahn showed up or didn't show up."

In one sense, Zander argues, the corporate raider was right: TWA could no longer be the kind of airline that catered to movie stars.

A critical weekend

Icahn's airline crashed in the early '90s. It wasn't all his fault. The recession, Iraq's invasion of Kuwait and the Gulf War combined to boost fuel prices and reduce travel. A proposed merger with Pan Am fell apart in 1991, as did a proposed purchase by California investor Kirk Kerkorian.

Icahn's selling of the profitable London routes, known as TWA's "crown jewels," led many to question the airline's future.

TWA announced in the summer of '91 that it planned to reorganize under a quickie "prepackaged" bankruptcy proceeding.

Meantime, the airline defaulted on tens of

A 1986 FLIGHT ATTENDANT STRIKE, CRUSHED BY ICAHN, ENRAGED WORKERS. (BELOW RIGHT) ATTENDANTS WORK OUT OF THE MACHINISTS UNION HALL. SAYS HERB JOHNSON (BELOW), FORMER MACHINIST PRESIDENT, "CARL ICAHN WAS STRICTLY A WALL STREET MONEY MERCHANT."

millions of dollars worth of bond interest payments and aircraft leases. It launched a big fare promotion for business flyers.

But the airline couldn't put its prepackaged bankruptcy together and filed for protection under a standard Chapter 11 bankruptcy in January 1992. A few months later, it was fighting for its life again in one of the toughest fare competitions in history.

That year almost became TWA's last. The airline had to get more employee concessions to survive. Icahn knew he was an impediment to talks. He also knew he could be on the hook for up to $1.2 billion in pension funding if TWA went out of business under his ownership.

He decided he must remove himself - the workers wouldn't give up more pay and benefits with Icahn around.

The unions hailed Icahn's departure, but they balked at the additional concessions that TWA and its creditors demanded. A long series of contentious talks ensued.

GLENN R. ZANDER

The talks reached a critical point the weekend of Aug. 22-23, 1992. The airline had decided it would shut down on Monday, Aug. 24, if it couldn't conclude a deal with the pilots and Machinists.

"We had no time," said Zander. "It wasn't like we could say, 'Oh, let's break for a week and come back,' because the money was going ... like a melting ice cube."

After 48 hours of nonstop phoning, faxing and posturing, a deal was clinched with the Machinists at 5 a.m. Monday. The pilots union climbed aboard at 6 a.m. TWA stayed in the air.

The workers agreed to 15 percent wage and benefit cuts over three years, and the creditors forgave about $1 billion in debts.

As part of the deal, Icahn, five months later, would send his $150 million to TWA, ending his tempestuous rule over the airline.

The king was dead.

A brief unity

On an emotional level, Icahn's departure provoked instant euphoria.

Morale zoomed. Union leaders who had railed against Icahn praised the new TWA. Zander and Robin H.H. Wilson, who had pulled an earlier stint as TWA's senior vice president of operations, took over with a feel-good management style.

With his British accent and fatherly manner, the Irish-born Wilson sounded like a wartime Winston Churchill, exhorting TWA employees to fight the good fight.

Former TWA spokesman Jerry Cosley said the workers loved Wilson, who was brought on board at the insistence of TWA's unions.

"Wilson knew all of their jobs in intimate detail and, maybe more importantly, understood their emotional dedication to the enterprise," Cosley said.

TWA introduced new "Comfort Class" seating to win back business travelers. Customers liked the longer leg stretch.

"It made flying on a business trip in coach class a treat rather than a trauma," said Kathryn Sudeikis, vice president of corporate relations for All About Travel in Mission.

TWA emerged from bankruptcy in November 1993, after nearly two years of grueling hearings and negotiations. It was now owned 45 percent by employees and 55 per-

A TWA MAINTENANCE BASE EMPLOYEE SPORTS A POST-ICAHN SWEATSHIRT: "WE'RE COMING BACK!" BUT THE AIRLINE CONTINUED TO SHRINK.

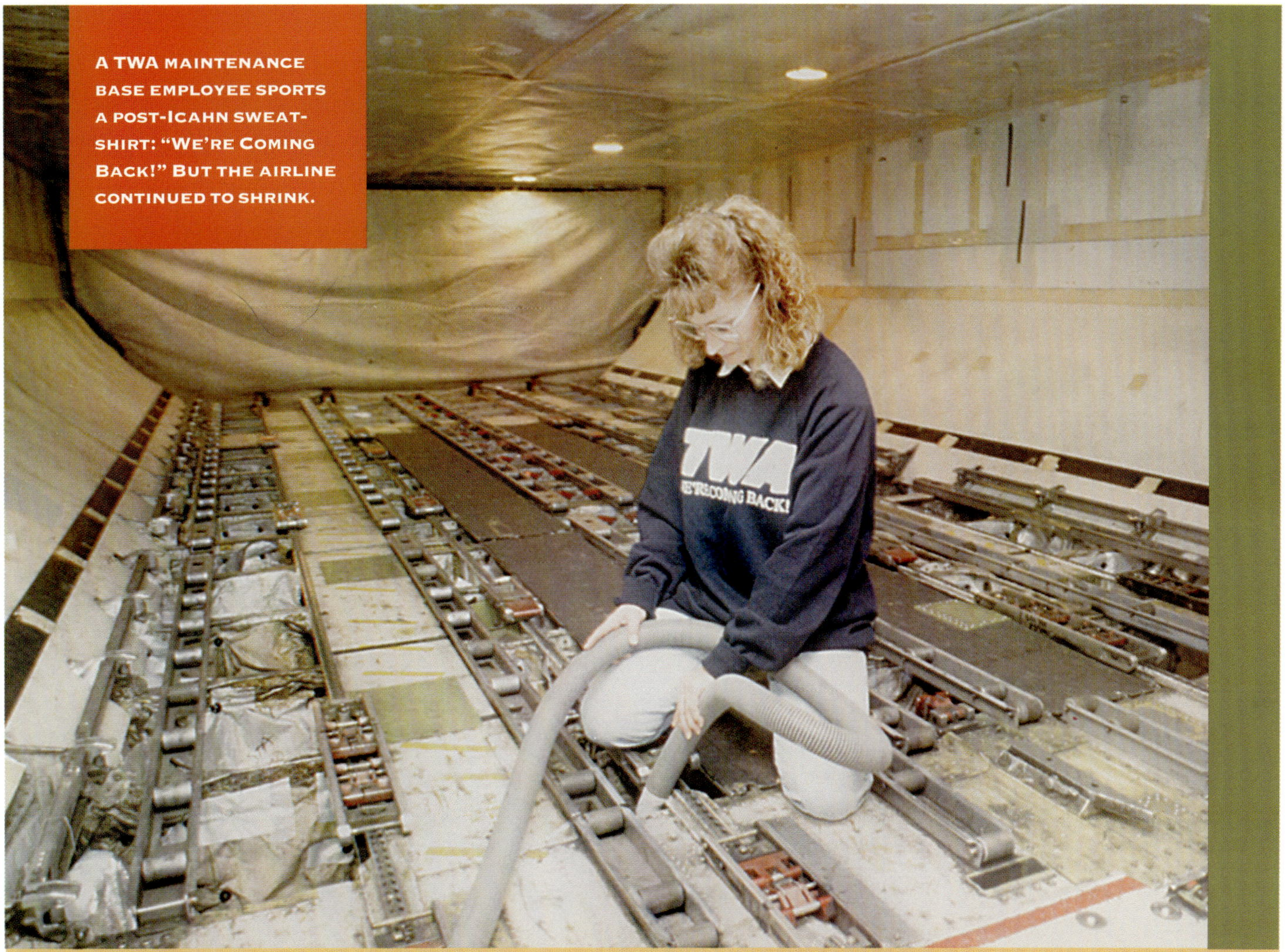

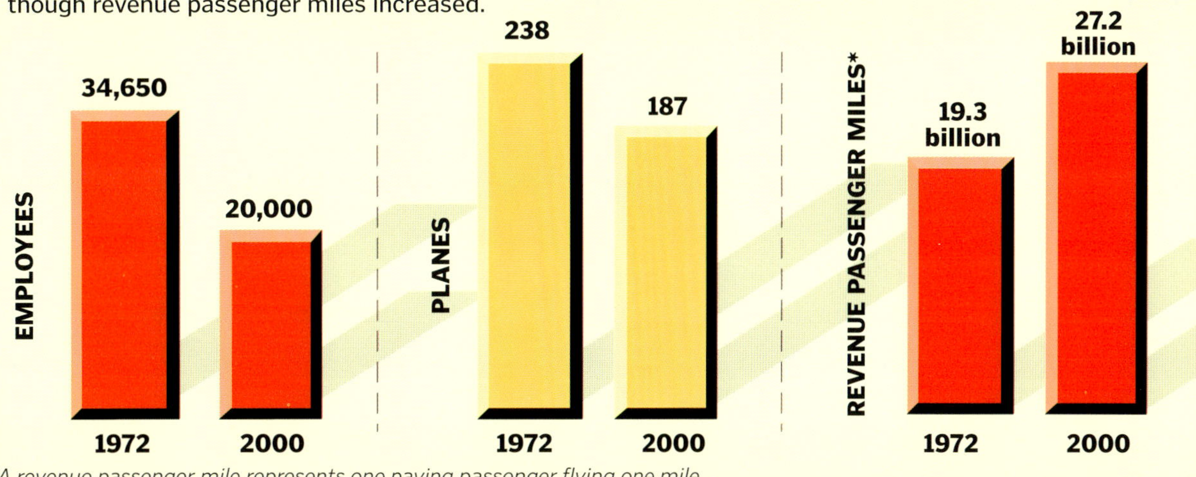

A leaner TWA

The airline industry as a whole grew in the latter part of the 20th century, but that came at the expense of some carriers, including TWA. The number of TWA employees and airplanes declined between 1972 and 2000, though revenue passenger miles increased.

*A revenue passenger mile represents one paying passenger flying one mile.

cent by creditors. It was a tremendous accomplishment.

But Icahn's farewell didn't solve everything for TWA. The airline, hobbled by a limited route structure and still burdened by huge debts, continued to lose money.

Despite all the talk of unity, the front office was soon squabbling over Comfort Class and other issues. TWA convulsed through a management shakeup in January 1994. William R. Howard was driven out after barely six months as chairman and chief executive officer. Zander quit after being denied his quest for the CEO post.

A new lineup emerged. Donald F. Craib Jr. replaced Howard. Jeffrey H. Erickson was hired as president and chief operating officer, later becoming CEO while Craib remained chairman.

Robert B. Cozzi, the TWA senior vice president of marketing who developed Comfort Class and other marketing innovations, quit over the airline's decision to put more seats on 10 jumbo jets. The workers' beloved Wilson was forced out as vice chairman in July 1994. Craib would later resign and be replaced by John C. Cahill.

With a financial crisis looming once again, TWA launched a massive restructuring in the summer of 1994. It said the plan that took it out of bankruptcy the year before was insufficient. It said it needed to slash costs and trim about $800 million off its $1.8 billion long-term debt.

Thousands of employees were laid off. Unions made more concessions. Creditors and aircraft lessors were asked to accept easier repayment terms. The carrier stopped making aircraft lease payments and cut off interest payments to holders of TWA notes.

On Nov. 1, 1994, TWA announced its first profit from operations in four years, though it continued to lose money at the bottom line. It made good strategic moves, such as getting rid of some unprofitable European routes while building up its St. Louis hub.

Then the restructuring effort seemed to flounder. The airline drew fire from its unions when it couldn't keep its promise to complete the makeover by the end of 1994. Talk of a new bankruptcy hurt ticket sales.

Talks dragged on with creditors and unions, who often squared off against one another. Employees, who took pay and benefit cuts and watched their friends get laid off, complained about executive bonuses.

But a consensus slowly forged.

Back to the future

TWA filed for its second bankruptcy on June 30, 1995. This time the move was greeted with relief, not distress.

The second bankruptcy was a true "prepackaged" bankruptcy, in which creditors had already agreed to the terms. TWA unburdened itself of about $500 million in debts. The creditors' stake in the airline rose from 55 percent to about 70 percent. The employees' stake dropped from 45 percent to about 30 percent. TWA's planes stayed in the air.

True to its word, TWA's second trip through bankruptcy court went quickly, with the airline emerging from bankruptcy in August 1995.

But expectations for the airline's future were mixed. Some industry analysts said TWA needed a merger partner to supplement its weak route system and aged, fuel-guzzling fleet.

The trouble, they said, was there were no appropriate suitors right then.

"It is possible they will make it, if the economy stays strong, if they are successful in arranging for new aircraft, if they are able to maintain good labor relations," Phillip Brannon, former associate director of Mabon Securities Corp. in New York said at the time. "But they have serious long-term problems, and they will not quickly go away."

Other observers were more optimistic. They said doomsayers often had TWA marching to the graveyard.

No one could deny that the cash-poor carrier faced more tough times. But for TWA, flying through tough times was much like a camel walking through desert - perfectly normal.

With as much hope as they could muster, TWA employees girded themselves for what lay ahead. ✳

WILLIAM HOWARD (ABOVE) WAS DRIVEN OUT AS CEO AFTER BARELY SIX MONTHS. (BELOW) A SPECIALLY PAINTED PLANE EMPLOYEES HELPED LEASE. (MIDDLE) THE NEW TWA DESIGN.

WHAT IF CRANDALL HAD STAYED?

TWA executive went on to lead American Airlines

Trans World Airlines in 1972 was one of the world's strongest air carriers. That's also when an intensely competitive workaholic was passed over for the job of chief financial officer.

The man was Bob Crandall, holder of an MBA degree from the University of Pennsylvania's Wharton School of business.

Crandall would eventually emerge as the visionary chief executive of American Airlines who would push American to embrace a deregulated, rough-and-tumble airline market faster and better than any other airline.

Observers say Crandall's departure from TWA was clearly an opportunity lost.

Airline analyst Morten Beyer says TWA would be today's industry leader had Crandall stayed.

"Crandall was quite an aggressive guy," Beyer said. "When people on the TWA board said 'Retreat,' Crandall would have said, 'Advance!'"

Before coming to TWA, Crandall had worked for Kansas City's Hallmark Cards, primarily in the credit and collections area of the finance department.

At TWA Crandall held several positions, including vice president of data processing at the carrier's financial operations center in Kansas City.

He promptly left TWA after losing out on the top finance job. After a short stint at the Bloomingdale's retail firm, he joined American Airlines, which was plagued with problems.

According to the book *The American Eagle, The Ascent of Bob Crandall and American Airlines* by Dan Reed, Crandall helped pull American back from the brink of bankruptcy in 1974.

He also helped invent the modern hub-and-spoke flight operating system.

And he oversaw the creation of SABRE, American's computerized reservation system, and led the airline to use computers in new ways.

"He saw the value of SABRE, not only for the travel agency industry to sell tickets, but as this powerful engine for gathering data about inventory control, which seats sold the best," biographer Reed, a business writer for the *Fort Worth Star-Telegram*, said in an interview.

Crandall also generated controversy. Known as "Fang" by his enemies, he peppered his speech with pervasive profanity. He was accused of illegal price-fixing and blamed for the failure of several competing airlines. He was vilified as an enemy of organized labor for creating a two-tiered wage scale at American.

Today, 29 years after Crandall cleaned out his desk at TWA, American is an industry powerhouse and is pursuing a plan to buy TWA out of its third bankruptcy proceeding.

Which begs the question: If TWA had hung on to Crandall and Crandall had become TWA's chief executive, would TWA be the reigning industry powerhouse?

Some airline experts think so, including one of the men who worked with Crandall.

"If he had been selected to be chief financial officer, it's clear that TWA would be the dominant carrier in America, as American is," said Bob McAdoo, a former TWA executive who co-founded People Express Airlines in 1980 and founded Kansas City-based Vanguard Airlines in 1994.

Crandall was McAdoo's boss at TWA in the early '70s, when McAdoo oversaw payroll and revenue accounting.

McAdoo said Crandall was

The American Eagle

The Ascent of Bob Crandall and American Airlines

Dan Reed

white shirts with the sleeves rolled up. His teeth were crooked and he frequently chewed on pencils. The man just didn't look polished.

But McAdoo also suspects another reason. "I think he was so much sharper than the top one or two guys at TWA at the time, they were probably afraid he'd outshine them," he said. "I think they were clearly not able to keep up with him in terms of his thoughts and his vision."

Crandall, who turned 65 in December 2000, retired from American in 1998. In an interview, he modestly declined to speculate on whether he could have built TWA into an airline resembling American.

"In fact, no one can tell how history would have come out," he said philosophically.

But Crandall didn't wax philosophic about the American-TWA deal.

"I was at American a long time (25 years), so my blood runs red, white and blue," he said. "I'm just pleased to see American doing well."

"one of these guys that was absolutely full of energy, absolutely straightforward. If he saw there was a problem to be solved, he would line us up and have us go directly at it. There was no politics, no cuteness. It was the equivalent of smash-mouth football."

Former airline executive Richard D. Pearson, who worked with Crandall at TWA and American, said he wasn't sure that Crandall alone could have given TWA the rocket boost it needed.

However, Pearson said Crandall knew the airline business "better than anybody in the industry the whole time I knew him. He knew how important computers were to the airline business."

So why was this hard-charging visionary passed over at TWA?

McAdoo said Crandall at that time had greasy hair and wore

 # THE FINAL APPROACH

The work week is over. On a Friday afternoon in February 2001, employees of the TWA overhaul base descend on the Final Approach Pub just off Interstate 29. They've come to throw back beers and talk about the years. ✸ *Airline memorabilia fill the place. Inflatable safety vests dangle above the bar, where five airline seats beckon. An "Arrivals/Departures" sign hangs near the pool room. A framed map of "The Lindbergh Line" rests on the floor.* ✸ *A dozen or so TWAers surround a table. Dick Hobbs has spent 33 years at the base. Charlie Lake, 34 years. Tom Johnson, in shipping and receiving, 23 years, only to be laid off five times.*

The topic this day is American Airlines' proposed buyout of their airline. "A good thing," says Johnson. "We're looking forward to being a secure company."

No more pink slips before Christmas? No more worries about the bank cashing your paycheck whenever TWA is in bankruptcy court? American Airlines is financially solid - the industry leader - and TWA is not, anymore.

In a perfect world these workers would keep wearing their TWA employee badges. But Gene Foster, the soft-spoken sage at the table, knows this isn't a perfect world.

"This is one tick in a 75-year clock," says Foster, who turned away from his college pursuits in philosophy, history and theology to help clean TWA's fleet. "This is the end. It's the last tick of an era. It's gone."

Not only could TWA's name vanish if American buys the airline, but so would Machinists Local 1650, which has represented TWA mechanics and related employees in Kansas City since 1946.

The union now has about 2,200 active members. They're outnumbered by retired members.

For sure, they would hate to see those red, slanted letters - "TWA" - disappear. But after years of turbulence, of pay cuts and crisis management, the gang at the Final Approach will trade tradition for the promise of security.

(ABOVE) TWA EMPLOY-EES TALK OVER THE NEWS OF AN AMERICAN AIRLINES BUYOUT AT THE FINAL APPROACH PUB. (BELOW) THE PIVOTAL LOSS OF TWA FLIGHT 800.

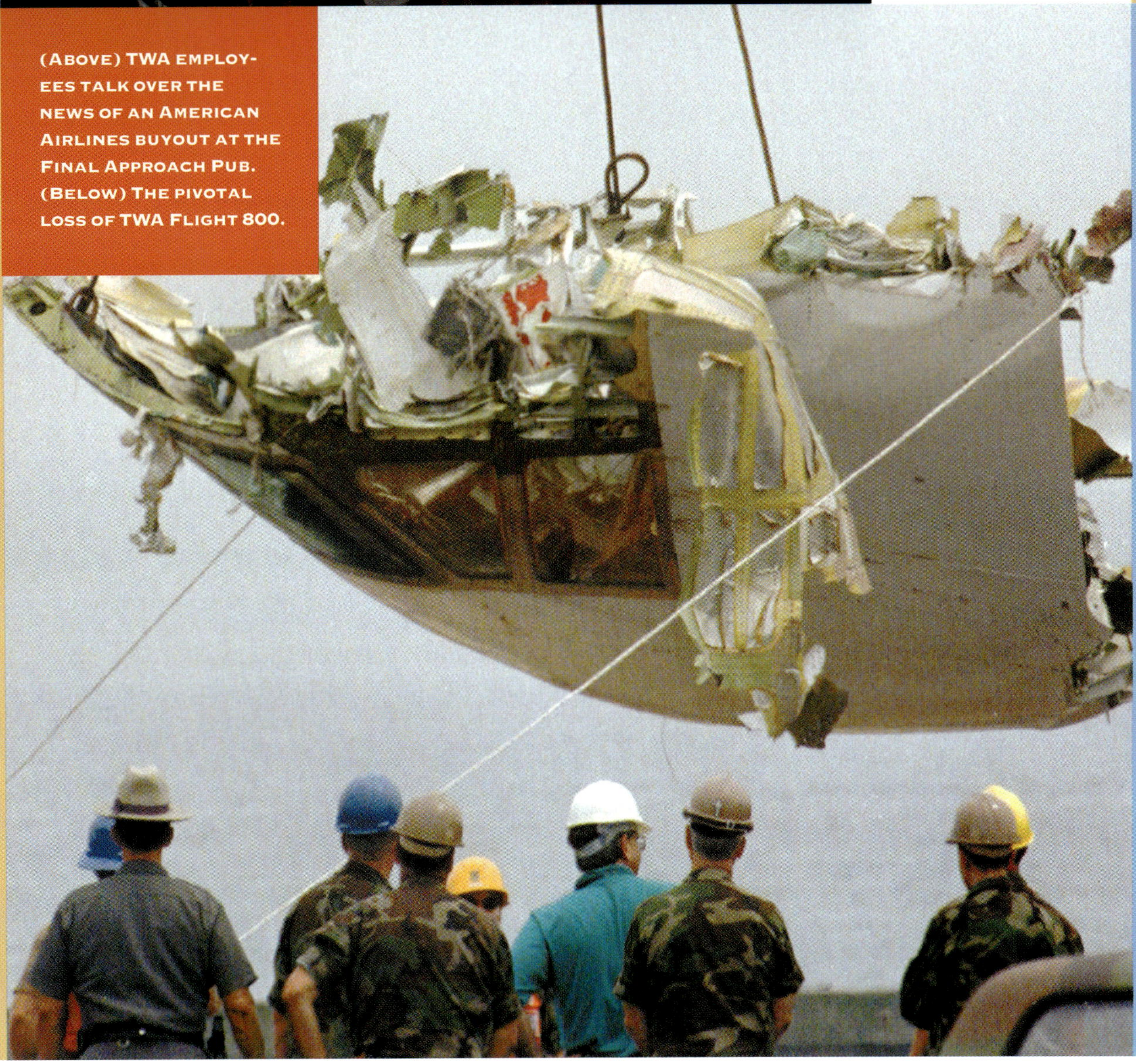

The bittersweet banter at the bar seemed far removed from August 1995, when a determined airline emerged from its second bankruptcy with big plans to succeed.

Fuel costs were tumbling. It was a good year for the industry.

The bankruptcy plan allowed TWA to unburden itself of $500 million of its $1.8 billion debt load. The company announced plans to modernize its fleet, to hire 2,100 new employees and to bring back nearly 200 who had been laid off from the overhaul base in 1992.

TWA issued common stock in 1995 and reported its first operating profit since the 1980s. A souped-up marketing campaign followed. It included co-sponsoring a Smithsonian Institution tour featuring an exhibit of TWA's dynamic history.

The city of St. Louis, where TWA moved its headquarters in 1994, became home to the Trans World Dome as the airline sponsored the new St. Louis Rams football stadium.

TWA's stock price hit a post-bankruptcy high of more than $23 in April 1996 - up from about $6 a share just six months earlier.

Then, mysteriously, a Boeing 747 bearing TWA's logo fell from the sky over the Atlantic Ocean off Long Island, N.Y.

The crash of TWA Flight 800 killed 230 passengers and crew. It happened July 17, 1996 - 42 years to the day after ground was broken for the Northland overhaul base. The

KANSAS CITY

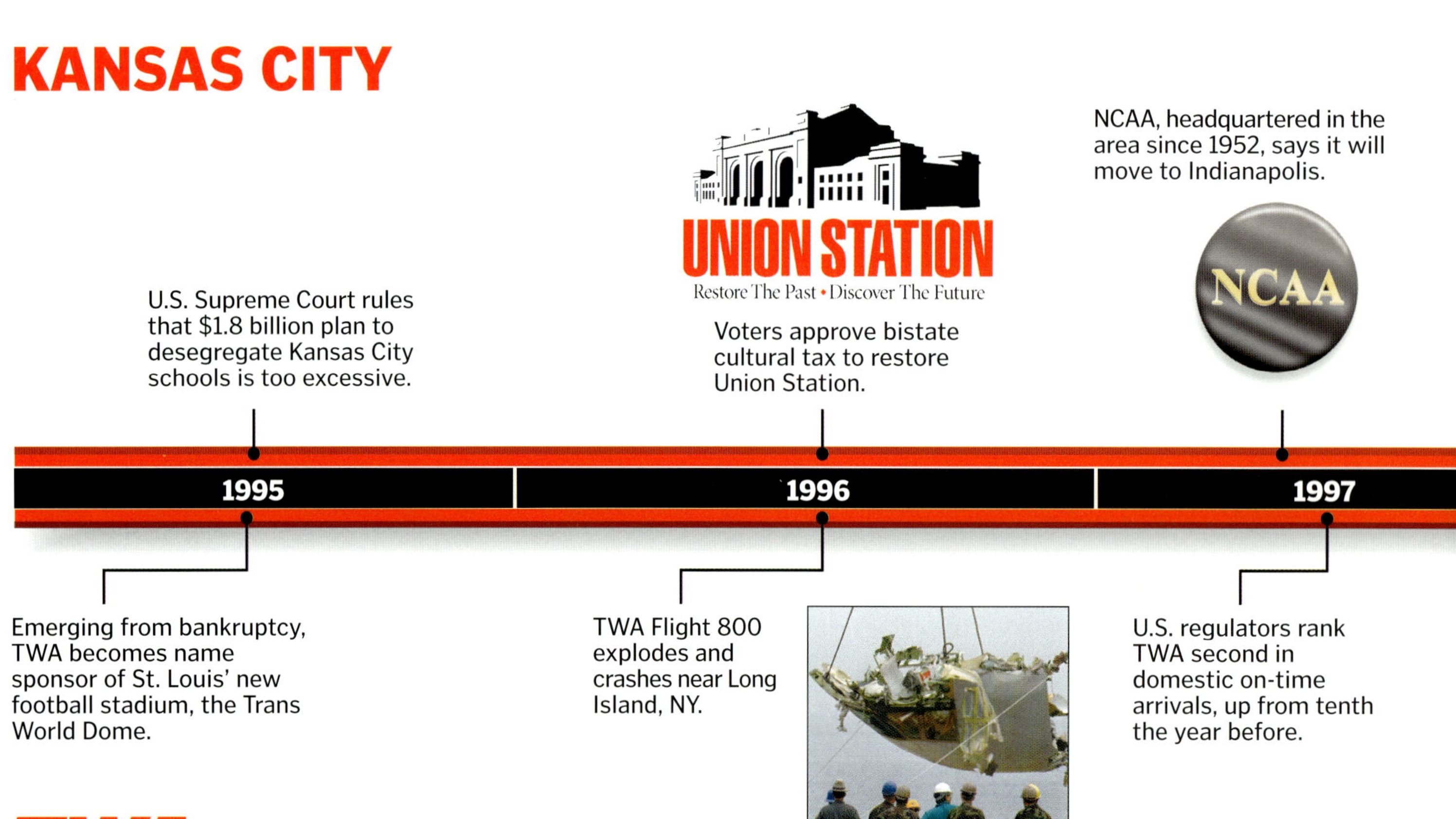

NCAA, headquartered in the area since 1952, says it will move to Indianapolis.

U.S. Supreme Court rules that $1.8 billion plan to desegregate Kansas City schools is too excessive.

Voters approve bistate cultural tax to restore Union Station.

1995 **1996** **1997**

Emerging from bankruptcy, TWA becomes name sponsor of St. Louis' new football stadium, the Trans World Dome.

TWA Flight 800 explodes and crashes near Long Island, NY.

U.S. regulators rank TWA second in domestic on-time arrivals, up from tenth the year before.

TWA

tragedy cast a pall over proud workers there who maintained an aging fleet.

"We take people's lives in our hands," mechanic Roger Tyler told *The Kansas City Star* at the time. "We don't take it lightly. I'll stand behind every pump I ever build."

Federal investigators moved toward a theory that a spark inside the fuel tank, caused perhaps by a short in wiring, made Flight 800 explode. The base workers rejected this as "impossible." Many argued the government might be covering up a military blunder, that Flight 800 was shot down.

Though official blame was never laid on TWA, nobody could deny the blow the airline took in its efforts to reverse course. Passenger bookings dropped. So did the value of TWA stock - back down to $6 a share by 1997.

Flight 800 "was massive negative publicity because it occurred in the New York media market - the media capital of the world," recalled Mark Abels, TWA's vice president of corporate communications, years later. He said the workers' morale suffered "for the better part of a year."

Still, again, the airline battled back.

At the end of 1998 TWA agreed to acquire 125 new planes, the biggest aircraft order in company history. "This will give TWA a modern fleet that is second to none," said Gerald T. Gitner, the chairman and chief executive officer at the time.

In fact, by 2001, TWA had transformed its

KANSAS CITY

Kansas City observes its 150th birthday.

A Celebration of the Heart

Renovation of Liberty Memorial wins voter approval.

Kay Barnes elected first woman mayor.

| 1998 | 1999 | 2000 | 2001 |

TWA announces plans to add 46 round-trip flights per week.

TWA takes delivery of new Boeing 717-200, orders 50 more.

Federal judge approves American Airlines' purchase of TWA over competing bid by Carl Icahn.

fleet from the industry's oldest to one of the youngest. The airline also improved its on-time performance, beefed up customer-service training and dropped some unprofitable European routes.

But all of the fine-tuning couldn't return TWA to its glory years. Hard as it tried, the airline hadn't posted an annual net profit since 1988.

"TWA waited too long," said former TWA executive Glenn R. Zander. "There wasn't enough time left, given their limited financing capabilities."

Zander, now the president of Aloha Airlines in Hawaii, said TWA was hampered by having only one flight hub - St. Louis. The airline was "too small to be a mega carrier and too big to be a niche carrier."

Turnover in the front office continued. Executives fought with directors. Former president and chief executive officer Jeffrey H. Erickson left in 1997. Gitner replaced him.

William F. Compton, former head of TWA's pilots union, became president and chief operating officer in December 1997. Groomed by Gitner for the next move up, Compton took the CEO job in 1999.

The airline kept hitting bumps on the labor front, too, as shaky relations continued with the Machinists union representing mechanics, flight attendants and others. Many of them "have become discouraged because of the way TWA has done business in the past," in areas such as employee givebacks on wages, said Butch Sponaugle, president of Local 1650.

Sponaugle said TWA planes always were kept in safe flying condition. But if an airline can't obtain parts in a timely manner, mechanics get frustrated.

What progress was achieved since the second bankruptcy "evaporated," Zander said, when fuel prices zoomed up again in 2000. Even with a newer and more efficient fleet, TWA's fuel costs jumped by $250 million in a year.

Abels described those costs as the "straw that broke the camel's back, though it was more like a ton of bricks."

Nevertheless, "the operational turnaround of TWA has been fantastic," he said after the news of American's offer to buy. "We've put TWA in a position where an airline like American can come in here and say, under the right circumstances, we see real value here...

"TWA people can take a lot of pride in that."

The sun dips to the horizon. There's time for one last round at the Final Approach.

"I'd rather work for TWA," shrugs mechanic Warren H. Ingram III. "But I'll work for American. It's a lot better than saying Icahn Enterprises, I'll tell you that right now."

No matter where the long, romantic and rocky ride of Trans World Airlines takes these workers, Ingram is certain of one thing. "In our blood, in our spirit," he says, they always will be TWAers.

Manager Kathy Woodward says the establishment is ready to add American Airlines knick-knacks to its decor. But she insists the bar will keep its red TWA sign, TWA china and assorted treasures salvaged from Kansas City's hometown airline.

Why hang on to it all?

"All of the retirees will still come in here," she says. "It will make them feel good." ★

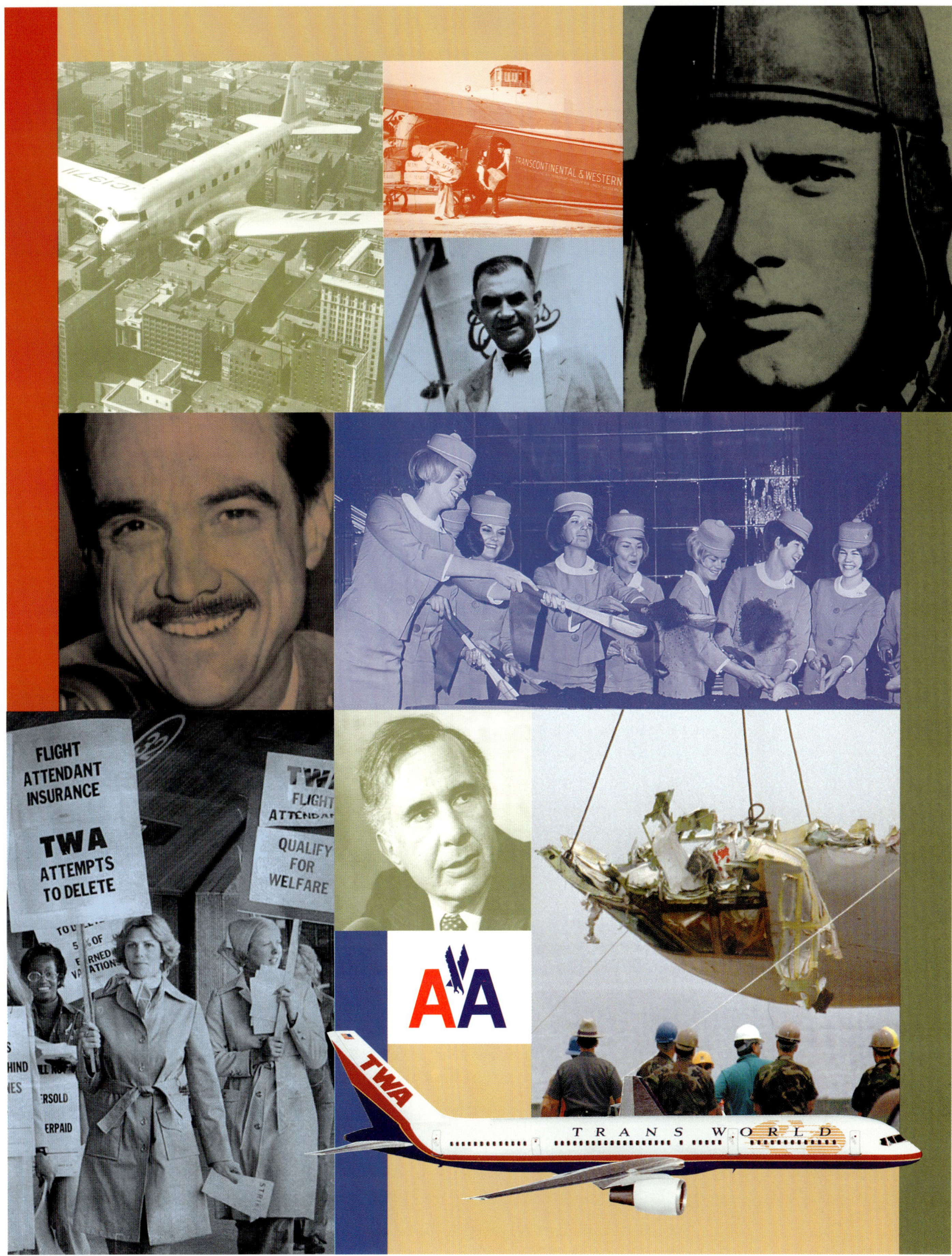

TRANSCONTINENTAL & WESTERN
FLIGHT
ATTENDANT
INSURANCE
TWA
ATTEMPTS
TO DELETE
TWA
FLIGHT
ATTENDANT
QUALIFY
FOR
WELFARE
AA
TWA
TRANS WORLD

Cover: TWA flight over Downtown Kansas City: *The Kansas City Star* archives.

Page 7: Charles Lindbergh: *The Kansas City Star* archives; Amelia Earhart: *The Kansas City Star* archives; "Kansas City" christening: *The Kansas City Star* archives.

Page 9: Gordon Parkinson: "The Making of An Airline"; overhaul base: *The Kansas City Star* archives; Howard Hughes: The Associated Press.

Page 11: TAT Tri-Motor: Transcontinental Air Transport; Lou Holland: Kansas City Museum.

Page 14: Charles Lindbergh: Pacific And Atlantic Photos Inc.

Page 15: Transcontinental & Western Air: *The Kansas City Star* archives. Log book: Johnna Flahive, *The Kansas City Star.*

Page 16: Charles Lindbergh: *The Kansas City Star* archives.

Page 17: Telegram: Kansas City Museum.

Page 19: Jack Frye: Tom Perry; passengers departing: Trans World Airlines promotional photograph; Ruth Molitor: "The Making of An Airline."

Page 23: Knute Rockne: *The Kansas City Star* archives.

Page 24: TAT plane and Constellation: Trans World Airlines promotional photograph.

Page 25: Howard Hughes: *The Kansas City Star* archives.

Page 27: Howard Hughes: *The Kansas City Star* archives.

Page 31: Lockheed Constellation: *The Kansas City Star;* twin-sized berths: Trans World Airlines promotional photograph

Page 32: Howard Hughes: The Associated Press.

Page 33: Fairfax Airport: *The Kansas City Star;* Fairfax flood: *The Kansas City Star;* Ralph Damon: *The Kansas City Star* archives.

Page 35: Maintenance base: *The Kansas City Star* archives; Constellation: Trans World Airline promotional photograph

Page 37: Wanda Moore and Katherine Grant: *The Kansas City Star.*

Page 38: TWA paper dolls: Johnna Flahive, *The Kansas City Star.*

Page 39: TWA hostesses: Trans World Airlines promotional photograph.

Page 40: Howard Hughes: The Associated Press.

Page 41: Howard Hughes top left: *The Kansas City Star* archives; top right: The Associated Press; bottom: The Associated Press.

Page 43: Hostesses: *The Kansas City Star;* Charles C. Tillinghast Jr.: *The Kansas City Star* archives.

Page 47: Baggage loading: *The Kansas City Star;* pilots and hostess: *The Kansas City Star* archives.

Page 48: Charles C. Tillinghast Jr.: Tom Dunn.

Page 49: TWA jets in a line: *The Kansas City Star;* splash: *The Kansas City Star;* TWA bottle: Johnna Flahive, *The Kansas City Star.*

Page 51: Phonograph courtesy of Tom Dunn.

Page 53: Boeing 747: *The Kansas City Star* archives; pumping fuel: *The Kansas City Star* archives; on strike: *The Kansas City Star* archives.

Page 54: Pin: Johnna Flahive, *The Kansas City Star.*

Page 55: Tom Perry: *The Kansas City Star.*

Page 57: Johnna Flahive, *The Kansas City Star.*

Page 59: Carl Icahn: The Associated Press.

Page 61: Jets for sale: *The Kansas City Star* archives; Richard D. Pearson: *The Kansas City Star* archives.

Page 65: Machinists picketing: *The Kansas City Star* archives; Carl Icahn: *The Kansas City Star* archives.

Page 67: Flight attendants on strike, top, bottom: *The Kansas City Star archives;* Herb Johnson: *The Kansas City Star archives.*

Page 68: Glenn Zander: *The Kansas City Star* archives.

Page 69: Maintenance base worker: *The Kansas City Star* archives.

Page 70: Jeffrey H. Erickson: *The Kansas City Star* archives.

Page 71: William Howard: The Associated Press; specially painted plane: *The Kansas City Star* archives.

Page 72: Bob Crandall: AMR Corp.

Page 75: Final Approach Pub: Johnna Flahive, *The Kansas City Star;* TWA Flight 800 wreckage: The Associated Press.